D0908473

# Handbook for Freelance Writing

**Michael Perry**

808.02
P464 h

2

**Library of Congress Cataloging-in-Publication Data**

Perry, Michael
Handbook for freelance writing / Michael Perry.
p. cm.
ISBN 0-8442-3255-6 (alk. paper)
1. Authorship. I. Title.
PN151.P47 1997
808'.02—dc21 97-287
CIP

Published by NTC Business Books, a division of NTC/Contemporary Publishing Company
4255 West Touhy Avenue
Lincolnwood (Chicago), Illinois 60646-1975 U.S.A.
© 1997 by NTC/Contemporary Publishing Company. All rights reserved.
No part of this book may be reproduced, stored in a retrieval system, or transmitted in any form or by any means, electronic, mechanical, photocopying, recording or otherwise, without the prior permission of the publisher.
Manufactured in the United States of America.

7 8 9 0 BC 9 8 7 6 5 4 3 2 1

24.95 AGN-5563

LIBRARY
MIAMI-DADE COMMUNITY COLLEGE
MIAMI

# Contents

## Chapter Four
## Commercial Writing 25



## Chapter Five
## Writing for Publication 41



## Chapter Six
## What Should I Write About? 51

# PREFACE

This is really only one story of thousands.

Freelance writing is a unique pursuit. Its practitioners are diverse, their methods even more so. Some write only for the "big names." Others write only commercial copy. Some dabble. Some are determined to survive solely on freelanced words.

There is no single path to follow.

And so, how did I choose my path through this book? First of all, the path reflects my freelance experience. Interpret what you read in that context. Second, the path may not be straight, but it is straightforward. There are no overblown guarantees, no discourses on subjects with which I have no practical experience. This book isn't about fame or angst or big book deals or the writer as heroic figure. It is a book about a fulfilling livelihood developed through individual combinations of spirit and craft; a livelihood that allows its practitioners the luxury of practicing survival by indulging a passion.

# CHAPTER ONE

# BEING A WRITER

Not long ago, I found myself on a university campus, facing a classroom of students majoring in education. I had been summoned and charged as follows: to say "something" about the writing process, and to share my thoughts on how these nascent teachers could make writing interesting to their students.

I began by telling them that a writer whose name I cannot recall once said our writing experiences are all formed by the age of 20. Along similar lines, Flannery O'Connor once said that anyone who has survived childhood has enough material to write about for the rest of his or her life. If these statements are true, I suggest it is because in those formative years we are affected directly by our observations and experiences. We have not yet established those filters with which we eventually impose a personal diffraction upon all perception. When we are young, new experiences dominate our attention in a way they never will after we develop preconceptions, prejudice, and preoccupations. And so, the importance of the role teachers play on young writers is crucial.

But how to charge students with the desire to write?

One option is to appeal to their basest instincts and incubating capitalist tendencies. When I speak to school children, I often lead off the session with a question: "How many of you are happy when your teacher gives you a writing assignment?" Much groaning and eye-rolling follows. At most, one child will raise a hand, and that child is generally bucking for promotion to milk monitor. Then I pose a follow-up question: "How many of you would be happy if your teacher gave you a writing assignment . . . and then *paid* you for it?" Hands shoot up like dog ears when a bone drops. Suddenly, the children understand and embrace the concept of freelance writing.

Of course, it is not nearly so simple.

## FOR LOVE OR MONEY

First of all, the likelihood an individual will be paid for writing—let alone eke out an existence through the stringing together of words—is slim. And I tell the children this. But there is a second point to be made. A point that goes beyond the issue of paying the rent, to address the very soul of the craft: A writer must love to write.

Distilled to its crass essence, this is a book about writing for money. I intend it to be fundamentally useful to that end. My editor rightfully demands it be so. And it is unlikely that you—as reader and customer—obtained this book simply to hear me rhapsodize about the fluttery feeling I get in my liver when I write a poem. But I can tell you without reservation that were the rewards for my persistence at the keyboard to be found solely in my checking account, I would have taken work running a backhoe (They're great . . . all those levers, all that dirt!) long ago. For all but a few freelancers, survival depends on the expeditious production of hack prose—a term I don't find offensive, by the way. Defined by turns as writing that is "routine or commercial" or "hackneyed; banal," *hack* is well-suited to describe a rather fair selection of my daily production. I'd love to join the literary pantheon, but in the meantime, the local hospital needs an 800-word piece on skin cancer and choosing a sunscreen. Hardly the stuff of literary legend, but writing nonetheless.

Professional musicians provide an encouraging analogy: In the beginning, they played weddings. Then they picked up a few concert dates. Eventually, they found themselves playing more concerts than weddings. And finally, when they hit their stride, they no longer needed to play weddings. But while they all cringe at the thought of ever again having to perform "Louie, Louie" to a room full of bad suits and undone cummerbunds, each and every one will tell you that those wedding dates laid the foundation of their careers. Those were the spots where they honed their "chops." Paying those dues prepared them for a chance at something more purely artistic; when opportunity came along, they were ready to give it a ride. And so, hack writing is the place to support yourself, the place to develop your own "chops." Hack writing is the writer's equivalent of playing weddings. I'd love to dispense with writing radio copy, or tips on how to avoid sunburn, but I'm not willing to dispense with my house payment, and I'm not willing to dispense with the progress I'm making toward working more and more on projects that truly move me—projects that truly allow me to *write.*

## ARE WRITERS BORN OR MADE?

When I stood before the education majors that day, I told them I would like to share with them my epiphany, that catalytic instant when I realized I wanted nothing more than to be a writer. But I don't have one. My arrival at this stage has been gradual, and at more times than I'd like to admit, an accident of fortune. I can, however, mark a few moments along that progression. One of the first was a book I pasted together detailing a trip to the zoo when I was but a sprout. It contained terse prose reminiscent of Hemingway's finest work, as I recall. Another was a three- or four-sentence, transparently autobiographical, short (and how) story about an elf. I plunked out the prose on Dad's old Underwood manual typewriter, and although I don't recall how old I was at the time, I do remember standing on the chair to reach the keyboard. But in retrospect, two assignments from my junior high English teacher may have done as much as anything to point me down this path.

Her name was Mrs. Rehrauer. Liz, actually, but forever Mrs. to me. I was in eighth grade when she came to our small rural school. It was her first teaching assignment, I believe, and I can remember a few details. That she brooked no sass, for instance. And that she allowed us to listen to a small FM clock radio while we scraped away at our writing. The volume was kept at a background level, and I remember Scott McCracken begging to turn it up when ABBA chirped through "Take a Chance on Me." We studied grammar, I'm sure, but as my editor will tell you, to this day I cannot diagram a sentence or give the definition of a split infinitive. Beyond visual echoes, I remember next to nothing of these lectures. But I remember two assignments very clearly. In one instance, Mrs. Rehrauer taped a black-and-white picture of an abandoned house to the chalkboard. "Today I want you to write a story that includes this house," she said. I imagine we looked at her with varying degrees of dumbfoundery. What kind of assignment was this? No particulars? No direction beyond a picture of an old wreck of a house? Several students (likely including me) questioned her further. Surely she wanted something more specific. As much as we may have chafed at assignments of structure, complete freedom opened a daunting void. But at some point I began to write, and soon I was not in a classroom, but on my way to an old wooden house. Rather than sweating over a correct answer, I was spinning an easy tale. For the first time, I was writing not as a student completing an assignment, but as a character telling a story; a contrived story, a bit of fiction, but a story I felt as strongly as truth.

The other assignment, described simply, was a free-verse poem. I still have it somewhere in a box I've U-Hauled through the years, and I assure you without needing to dig it out and read it again that it is awful beyond even the mitigating effects of nostalgia. Nonetheless, for the first time since I'd gnawed on a pencil, I was given a peek at the enchanting possibilities of words. Of my power over them, and their power over me. Of the possibility of creation without constraint. It didn't set me on fire, but it set a spark. I learned that writing could transcend the tedious to become sensuous. And there are times, even now, when my fingers find a rhythm on the keyboard and the words roll across the screen like a parade of ants headed for a jam jar, when writing is just that: sensuous. It comes so easily. Rough, yes, and unpolished, and maudlin and immature and in need of a good tamping down, but unleashed, unfettered, and uninhibited.

Mrs. Rehrauer did something far more important than teach me to hunt down split infinitives or stomp on comma splices; she invested writing with emotion.

## THE WRITING LIFE

The title "writer" is freighted with a myriad of images and connotations: The pale, tortured scrawler, musing away in the garret, brow ribbed with thought, scribing the wisdom of the ages upon curling parchment. The troubled thinker, driven to drain her very soul and strain the juice for truth. The ranter, hurling his rage against the page. And if each and every one of us will just admit it, there is a part of us strongly desirous that others look at us and see someone whose back is a bit bent by the pen, brow furrowed by deep thought.

Many of the students I meet think of writers in terms of serious, dry folk. Or serious, dry *dead* folk. I love to tell them otherwise. Not all writers are pale and tortured. It is not necessary to huddle in a darkened aerie, cranking out angst. Recent writing assignments have taken me to fire stations in Central America, a Swiss country music festival, on the road with a traveling butcher, and to the Nashville farm of a muscle-bound country music star. I've shadowed professional football players (that's a lot of shadow, folks), turned green in the seat of an aerobatics plane, and snuck into a Bill Clinton press conference. Of course, in between trips, I huddle in my darkened aerie and crank out angst. Or brochure text exalting a residential home for the elderly.

The point is that the spectrum of writerly occupations is a wide one: screenwriter, poet, news stringer, journalist, CD-ROM scriptwriter, novelist, teacher, copywriter, hack. Wherever you see words, you see the tracks of a writer. Most writers can be found at several points along the spectrum simultaneously. This year, in the same month that I published a "sensitive" essay in a glossy nature magazine, I wrote three pizza commercials.

## REALITY

As a writer along that spectrum, you must strike a balance between writing to write and writing to pay the bills. And as a writer, that's what I hope to do in this book. I want to touch on the fulfilling artistry of words, but also point out their use as salable materials of commerce. I want to encourage, but I also promise to be frank. It is up to you to establish the nature and level of writing you wish to pursue. Do you want to write strictly for personal fulfillment? For occasional publication? For a living?

If you choose to write for a living, don't pitch your day job. Ease your way into the field. In an article for *Writer's Digest,* Kenneth Henson wrote, "Since writing's pay generally parallels any author's skill level, it's better to put aside the concern for money until some success has been reached." Very true. However, remember that the definition of success is highly individual. I've been freelancing for several years, and if I defined success as having my name bandied about by prominent editors and publishers, I'd still be proofreading brochures for legal seminars (the day job that nurtured me through my early days). But I defined—and continue to define—success as a freelance income adequate to pay the rent and buy groceries.

If you choose to write purely for your own enjoyment, and view sales of your writing as a pleasant bonus, more power to you. Just make sure you've got a little something on the side to tide you over until the book deal comes in (see "Before You Quit . . ." sidebar).

Finally, amidst all this idea of craft and commerce, allow yourself time to write for yourself. To write what you feel; things that have nothing to do with freelance assignments, things you need show no one. I show my stuff to anybody I can corner at this point, but for years I kept it all out of sight. In writing for yourself, you will reinforce the most important lesson of all: Writing in its purest, most unpretentious form has nothing to do with the pen, and everything to do with the soul.

## WHAT ABOUT THAT DAY JOB?

I was lucky. I found a day job (proofreading) that allowed me to work with words. It was also a job that was easily left at the office. At night, I could write, knowing full well that whatever faced me at work the next morning didn't require my preoccupation outside the hours of 7:30 A.M. to 4:30 P.M. Not everyone pursues day jobs of such simplicity. The great poet Wallace Stevens was an insurance executive all his life. And based on one of my favorite anecdotes of understatement, he didn't moon about the office, bemoaning his "day job" as an unwelcome hindrance. When a writer showed up to research a biography on this giant of modernist poetry, a surprised coworker is reported to have said, "Wally wrote *poetry*?!" Chaucer was a shipping clerk; T.S. Eliot was a bank clerk; William Carlos Williams was a country doctor.

Some writers seem to feel that having a "day job" robs them of a measure of literary cachet. If that's your feeling, I recommend you identify a few of your favorite cachet-emitting writers. With mighty few exceptions, you'll find out they all have a day job of some sort. Poets in particular seem to come equipped with a high cachet quotient, and yet, odds are, if you track down a high-cachet versifier, you'll end up at a university, where that poet will be employed as a professor. In other words, working a day job.

It's unrealistic to think you can launch your freelance career without weaning yourself with a day job. Based on my experience, a day job that's not overtaxing on the brain or lets you work with words—or both—is perfect. In order to conduct interviews or research, or meet with clients, you'll need flexibility; you might consider a "day job" in which you work nights or weekends. Some folks theorize that your day job should be as far removed from writing as possible. Their line of thinking is that the more you give of your writing self at the day job, the less is left for your own writing. I'm not convinced, but am prepared to admit it probably depends on the type of person you are.

And what about taking that final plunge? When do you leave the day job? Again, I was fortunate. My proofreading job had evolved into a more wide-ranging position and allowed me flexibility. I was also able to taper from full time to part time. Furthermore, I was a single person with a college degree in a field that at that time was constantly hiring. I had a net. And so, based on an increasing number of sales and a few relatively regular assignments, I simply took the step. You may wish to be a bit more scientific. Sit down and look at the numbers. How much income do you need to survive? Are you willing to simply survive? Are you prepared to give up the comfort of a regular (small though it may be) paycheck in return for irregular and uncertain income? Do you have all the equipment you need? What about health insurance? How will you plan for retirement?

One sensible thing I did was wait until I had enough money in the bank to survive for at least six months. And I did dip into those funds in the first year. Took 'em right down to triple digits, as I recall.

Here's the bottom line: To this day, I consider myself six months to a year away from a day job. There are no guarantees. You may be driven to write, but you are required to eat. And for all its desirability, cachet simply isn't filling.

## Before You Quit Your Day Job . . . Read This!

If you're pondering the freelance leap, I recommend you read "Freelancing Full-Time," an article by Sally-Jo Bowman in the November 1996 issue of *Writer's Digest.* While I am unmoved by her recommendation that your first step be the crafting of a personal "mission statement" (I consider them overearnest frou-frou that distracts from the grunt work at hand), Ms. Bowman's straightforward and well-thought-out approach will help you make an informed decision. Well, an informed gamble, anyway.

# CHAPTER TWO

# THE SECRETS TO SUCCESS

First, let's dispense with the bad news: There are no secrets. There are no Ten Sure-Fire Steps to Success. There are no courses, connections, contacts, or computer programs that will guarantee your ability to make a living as a writer. There are only words, and your ability to arrange them.

## A WRITER MUST WRITE

> "If one wishes to be a writer, one shouldn't talk about it, one should do it."
>
> *—Louis L'Amour (more on him later!)*

Above all else, you must write. If you do not write, you are not a writer. It really is that simple. You have to plant your posterior in the chair and pound the keys. Over the years, I have run into platoons of people who profess to be writers. They can talk at length about their writerly dreams, aspirations, and troubled souls. Over these same years, I fear I have come to believe that deep down inside (or perhaps much closer to the surface) most don't want to be a person who writes; they want to be a person who *talks* about writing.

I for one certainly find it easier to talk about writing than to actually perform the feat. Although I lack the lexicon of academia necessary to fool anyone for any great length of time, I can hold my own with the best of them if the hour is late and writing is the topic. And I *enjoy* talking about the process of writing. It's a wonderful, personal thing, writing, and surrounded by the right people, we like to share wonderful, personal things. Even a stoic Scandinavian type such as myself, my tongue quickened with caffeine, discretion suspended by the late hour, and my mind fuddled with other people's cigarette smoke, will prattle at length about the visceral thrill of the process of creation—from the animate touch of the keyboard when you're in the groove, to the interminable chiseling and scraping required when the muse is in a more parsimonious mood.

But none of this makes us writers. Conversationalists, perhaps. Actors, more likely. But writers? No. Writers write. It is only through writing that you can discover if you are a writer. It is only through writing that your writing strengths are discovered. It is only through writing that your writing *weaknesses* are revealed.

Pardon my vernacular, but whether it's an opus or a 250-word profile for the local business weekly, it ain't writ 'til it's wrote. No matter how much you prepare, no matter how much you talk, no matter how much coffee you drink, it isn't written until words—selected and pressed into service by you—are affixed to a readable medium.

Before writing becomes a noun, it must be a verb.

## WRITE EVERY DAY

Lee Gutkind is a professor of English at the University of Pittsburgh, the editor of *Creative Nonfiction,* and the author of eight nonfiction books. He's got it made, I'd say. A fellow like that can pretty much coast.

Not so.

In "The Essayist at Work," a special issue of *Creative Nonfiction,* Gutkind writes, "Writing is a difficult labor, in which a regular schedule, a daily grind of struggle, is inevitable." Lest you think those are simply artful words—don't. Gutkind rises at 5 A.M. every morning. To write. He might work on a current project, he might write in his journal, or he might write a letter. But he writes (see "Write *What* . . ." sidebar). Long-distance runners have long reported experiencing "runner's depression" as a result of skipping their daily run. Gutkind is a runner as well as a writer, and he says missing a day of writing evokes a feeling similar to runner's depression. "Pick your best time, and then force yourself to get in that habit," says Gutkind. "You've got to write."

Allow me to invoke the example of musicians once again: My friend Andy is a professional guitarist. Through the years, we have spent time on the road together. Wherever we go, he takes one of his guitars along. At some point during a long drive, he will pull the instrument out of its case and noodle away. Accompanying him on tour in Europe, I would return to the hotel room to find him rehearsing runs of music on an unplugged electric guitar. When I left that tour, I was joined on the train from Geneva to Paris by another guitarist from the tour. He was going to visit a friend, and was traveling light. His performance guitars had been flown home with the rest of the band. But he carried with him a Martin Backpacker®, an abbreviated version of a guitar designed to fit in a backpack. Even while living out of a pack, he continued to practice his craft.

Both of these musicians are well established. Apart from concert settings, they long ago got over the need to pull out a guitar simply to draw attention to themselves. They play every day, on the road and off, because they respect their craft. Because they have never lost that hunger to become better. Because they know the learning curve describes an infinite arc. It is the same with writing.

Of course, if you are a freelancer, the impetus to write every day is twofold. First, you write every day in order that you may continue to become a better writer. Second, you write every day in order that you may continue to eat.

### WRITE *WHAT* EVERY DAY?

Many writers keep a journal. Lee Gutkind keeps a personal journal and a writer's journal. I don't keep a regular journal, but I have a massive file in my computer in which I journal (verb) when I feel moved to do so or feel I need to capture an event in some form. I am pretty good about keeping a daily journal when I travel, and not just as a writerly indulgence. I've referred to my travel journals several times for articles and essays, and let's face it: The romantic in all of us loves the idea of sitting on a hotel balcony in Central America, or over a fresh cup of tea in England, or beneath a tent on a rainy day in Norway, scribbling away. While these settings often elicit useless ramblings—the equivalent of poorly focused vacation slides—they are often the source of critical detail when you're back at your word processor.

But back to the topic at hand. Writing every day doesn't have to mean "journaling." It can mean composing query letters asking editors for assignments or proposing article ideas. When you write a query letter, you're accomplishing a necessary and vital freelance task (read *chore*), while simultaneously sharpening your ability to write well.

Writing every day can mean composing a letter to a friend, as Gutkind does when he can't seem to get anything going in his two journals. I find letter writing to be a great exercise in limbering up the fingers and loosening up the brain so that the ideas can roll out. And of course, writing every day includes your work to meet deadlines.

The point is, a day should not pass when you do not in some way herd some words.

## THE MYTH OF INSPIRATION

> "I write when I'm inspired, and I see to it that I'm inspired at nine o'clock every morning."
>
> —*Peter De Vries*

Waiting for inspiration to strike before writing is like waiting for inspiration to strike before breathing. Freelance writers (most writers, for that matter) do not thrive on inspiration. Inspiration is a luxury affordable only to writers with an inheritance or an especially long prison term.

I am not dismissing the concept of inspiration. I believe in its existence—or at least in the general concept. The term itself has an archaic ring, but for the sake of discussion, I do believe that there are times when inspiration strikes; when the words come quickly, leaping from the keys *tempo allegro,* the rhythm so lively you fear you will fall behind and lose the frequency. Some writers claim they are merely "channeling" in these situations, that they are being "given" the words. I'm not so sure about that, but the bottom line is this: Whether it's channeling or simply a fortuitous set of chemical reactions in the old brain, inspiration provides limited returns, and as a writer serious about craft, you can't afford to wait around for it. What you can do, however, is be ready for it. Write every day. Keep your writerly engine running, and when inspiration shows up, you can take it for a ride.

### Albert Payson Terhune on Inspiration

Albert Payson Terhune has an interesting take on inspiration:

> "I have learned, as has many another better writer, to summon inspiration to my call as soon as I begin my day's stint, and not to hang around waiting for it. *Inspiration* is merely a pretty phrase for *the zest to work.* And it can be cultivated by anyone who has the patience to try. Inspiration that will not come at its possessor's summons is like a dog that cannot be trained to obey. The sooner both are gotten rid of, the better." (Quoted from *Writer's Digest,* June 1930.)

## HOW READING AFFECTS WRITING

Want to write good stuff?

*You must read.*

First, you must read for yourself. I'm not an academically prepared writer; I have a bachelor's degree in nursing, for Pete's sake. I consider myself a dilettante. I keep waiting to get caught; for someone to say, hey wait a minute, this guy's *faking* it! Not only am I not well-versed in the academics of literature, I can barely hum the chorus. When I'm in literary company, I feel the impostor. I have the greatest respect for those with an understanding of the mechanics and theory of writing, regardless of the genre. I can't diagram a sentence. I can't define the terms *split infinitive* or *comma splice.* But I can string together generally acceptable prose. Why? I have to believe it's a result of reading.

I grew up reading voraciously (we didn't have a television; I still don't). Not all the classics, mind you. I survived on a pretty heavy diet of Louis L'Amour cowboy books and outdated copies of *Sports Afield.* And I still read. I read to learn the craft of writing. Joan Didion once said grammar was a piano she played by ear, and I hope some day I can thank her personally for that quote, because it was a breakthrough realization for me. Reading helps me write by ear.

In his essay "The 5 Rs of Creative Nonfiction," *Creative Nonfiction* editor Lee Gutkind casts reading in the role of the fourth "R":

> Not only must writers read the research material unearthed in the library, but they also must read the work of the masters of their profession . . . almost all writers have read the best writers in their field and are able to converse in great detail about the stylistic approach and intellectual content.

I have also heard Gutkind suggest that a writer should read in the way an architect looks at a building. You or I see a building; the architect sees the blueprint, the superstructure, sees how it is all put together.

Finally, you must read the publications you want to write for. I can go on chapter after chapter about how to write the perfect opener, how to construct the body of the piece, when and how to use quotes to greatest effect, how to draw a reader's attention through the use of bulleted items, and etc., but in the end, there is no guide but the actual market. If you're putting together a 100-word piece for *The New York Times Magazine,* you don't need to read my section on writing witty leads, you need to read twenty-five 100-word pieces in *The New York Times Magazine.* If you want to write a profile for *Spy,* you must read *Spy,* steep yourself in *Spy*'s irreverence, school yourself in *Spy*'s editorial take. And so on.

I'll share what I know, tell you what I think, point you in a certain direction, save you the occasional misstep. But nothing replaces reading.

## ARM YOURSELF WITH EXPERIENCE

> "Stand up and live before you sit down and write."
>
> —*Henry David Thoreau*

> "A writer should know something well, and it shouldn't be writing."
>
> —*Randall Jarrell*

Collect experience and observation. Nothing makes a writer like experience. Distilled to its essence, experience means people, places, and things. The more people you meet, places you see, and things you do, the better writer you will become. The more you observe, the more your writing will take on unique character.

Asked about the wide range of topics he skewers, humorist P. J. O'Rourke once self-deferentially described himself as a "witty generalist." Taking a cue from P.J., I describe myself as a "witless generalist." That is, I don't know a lot about any one thing, but I know a little about many things. Chances are, when an editor approaches me about a topic, I'm not an expert, but I have a good idea about where to initiate a connection. More important, the wider my experience, the more likely I am to be able to propose article ideas of interest to that editor.

Experience comes in many forms and yields unexpected rewards. I was raised on a small dairy farm in rural Wisconsin. I worked my way through college as a ranch hand in Wyoming. I've worked on a sawmill, helped build houses, and run a wheelbarrow. Because of these experiences, I love assignments that put me in contact with folks who bend their backs, use their hands to put food on the table. Even though I'm no truck driver, I've done just enough truck steering (there's a difference, as all truck *drivers* will tell you!) to know what it takes to do the job. I know better than to overmythologize the virtues of hard work, and yet I understand the satisfaction it brings, and attempt to capture that feeling when I write about it. When I write an essay, it is very likely to be informed by that blue-collar perspective.

I have a bachelor's degree in nursing. It has been many years since I worked as a nurse, but I remain familiar with the profession, and my writing resume reflects this. I write patient profiles for an in-house hospital publication, in which it is critical that I provide medically accurate information in terms understandable to a lay person. I write chapters for a medical/legal textbook company. For these assignments I must be able to wade through volumes of professional journals, accurately consolidating information in terms understandable by non-medical professionals. I have cowritten articles for professional nursing journals, assisting nurse researchers whose research skills outstrip their writing skills. Each of these assignments can be traced directly back to my experiences as a nurse. While I left nursing behind as a profession, I did not leave it behind as a source of writing income. Nor have I left it behind as a source of material. The experiences I accrued as a nurse have shown up in essays, poetry, and short stories.

Whatever your experience, consider how it can inform your writing. It is a valuable source for reasons practical (it can help you establish a niche), and reasons artistic (it establishes style). It's not necessary that you spend the next twelve years actively pursuing "experience" as if it were arranged in the manner of a checklist. Every sentient being has experience by virtue of existence. Your task as a writer is to reach an understanding of how your experience can serve and inform your craft.

### Edward Abbey on Experience

"I don't think a college degree is necessary to become a good writer. I'm not even certain it's an advantage. College probably won't *hurt* you—if you don't take it too seriously. But far more important, I believe, is broad general experience: living as active a life as possible, meeting all ranks of people, plenty of travel, trying your hand at various kinds of work, keeping your eyes, ears and mind open, remembering what you observe, reading plenty of good books, and writing every day—simply writing."

*—Edward Abbey (quoted from* Writer's Digest, *October 1988)*

## PAY ATTENTION

Of course, simply experiencing things is not enough. Consider the words of poet Bruce Taylor:

*Pay attention.*
*This is everything.*
*Pay attention.*

One poem, three lines. And for my money (mostly pennies in an old shampoo bottle), the finest bit of advice a writer can get. Experience is nothing if you fail to pay attention. Pay attention to what the experience means beyond the experience. Pay attention to the possibilities opened by the experience. Pay attention to those things others miss. Pay attention to things apparently of little use. Pay attention today with an eye toward tomorrow. Pay attention to your writing. Pay attention to the writing of others.

Pay attention.

## PERSEVERE

Just as I am leery of inspiration, I am leery of inspirational quotes. But when they say what I mean better than I can say it, I'll use them. And so, it's time to trot out that champion of bootstrappery, our 30th president, he of the original frosty mug, the irrepressible Calvin Coolidge:

> "Nothing in this world can take the place of persistence. Talent will not; nothing is more common than unsuccessful men with talent. Genius will not; unrewarded genius is almost a proverb. Education will not; the world is full of educated derelicts. Persistence and determination alone are omnipotent. The slogan 'press on' has solved and always will solve the problems of the human race."

Perhaps that final line is a touch optimistic; never mind, we're not about the business of solving the problems of the human race. But when it comes to freelancing, persistence is your ace in the hole. Persistence will elevate your talent, draw attention to your genius (should you possess it), and—to an extent—make up for your lack of education. Note I said it will *elevate* talent, not *substitute* for talent, but make no mistake: Simply by being persistent, you can set yourself apart from the crowd of writers who aren't strapped in for the long haul. We've all heard stories of the writer whose blockbuster book was rejected by every publisher in business, save one. Anyone who freelances successfully can supply the analogous experience; an article placed after rejections in the double figures. As in baseball, there is room in the freelancing world for utility players. For writers blessed not with transcendent prose but with a tenacious work ethic. Good writing comes first, but persistence runs a photo-finish second.

I like the way Bob Bly puts it in his book, *Secrets of a Freelance Writer:*

> You have to be reasonably intelligent to be a writer, I suppose. But not brilliant. Intellectual curiosity and enthusiasm are far more important than sheer brainpower when it comes to being a good and successful writer.

Translated, Bly's "enthusiasm" is Coolidgean persistence.

## CULTIVATE CONNECTIONS

"All right," you're saying, "cut to the chase. In writing, as in most things, it all boils down to whom you know."

Well, yes. But stay with me on this one.

The idea of cultivating "connections" is distasteful to most writers. Images of grinning toadyism prevail. The inference is that positioning takes precedence over ability. And to an extent, this is true. In a very forthright statement made while participating in a recent panel discussion, *Vogue* senior editor Barbara Jones told the audience of writers that frankly, "schmooze factors and connections are a reality." But the connections you need to make it as a freelancer are rarely the schmoozy type; neither are they as unattainable as you might think. And whether they be with local commercial clients or the highfalutin editors of big-time magazines, you *will* need to establish connections. After all, as a man I know only as Campbell once said:

> "People who want milk should not seat themselves on a stool in the middle of a field in hopes that a cow will back up to them."

I live in a tiny, rural Wisconsin farming community. My odds of making "connections" are certainly not those of a perky Yale grad doing a stint as an intern at *The New Yorker.* But over time, they are not necessarily less. Connections are an accumulation of contacts; that accumulation takes place over an accumulation of time. The most fruitful connections aren't of the slap-on-the-back, let's-do-lunch variety. They are respectful and collegial, and based on confidence earned through delivery of good writing. Every writer disheartened by Barbara Jones' straightforward reference to schmooze should take heart from her follow-up comment: ". . . but always, it comes down to good work."

And so, the person who can most help you with your writing career isn't perched in a New York penthouse or wafting through a cocktail party of publishing's high and mighty. The person who can most help you with your writing career is holding this book.

## Janice Holt Giles on What Makes a Writer

> "I have no convictions about whether writers are born or made. Maybe it's a little bit of both. I would guess you must be born articulate and imaginative, then learn the techniques of the trade. But I do have some strong convictions about what makes a durable professional writer. First, he wants to write more than he wants to do anything else in the world. He wants to write more than he wants to party and play, travel, earn more money more easily, gain prestige and power in any other field. I don't know why anybody should, but the genuine article, the real producing writer, does.

"Next he is persistent. He is almost totally undiscourageable. Rebuffed by one editor he plods on to another. He doesn't give up easily. In fact he doesn't give up at all. He's in there fighting all the time. If he did give up, he'd never get published.

"Third, he is capable of very hard work and very lonely work for very long periods of time. When he sits down to begin a book he voluntarily makes a jailbird out of himself for a year, two years, maybe three. He does it knowing that he has turned the key himself. Nobody asks him to write that book, but he has to and he knows the only way to do it is to go to his desk every morning, every week, every month until he has come to the end. All producing and selling writers have this quality of self-discipline, for nobody is boss and nobody sets a time clock for them and nobody really cares whether they write or not."

*—Janice Holt Giles,*
*("Welcome to Cathay," in*
A Little Better than Plumb*)*

# CHAPTER THREE

# Who Wants My Writing?

I don't know much about art. I know I don't much care for paintings of children with oversized eyes, or dogs who play poker, but neither do I "get" Picasso. But as writers living in an uncertain time for writers, I think we can take a lesson from the New York art world—my observations about which I base entirely upon a single article in *The New York Times Magazine.*

During the 1980s, the New York art scene flourished. Great sloshing gobs of money (present, according to the article, thanks to Reaganomics) fueled an elite boom (yes, I suspect money, which allows one to buy art regardless of an ability to appreciate art, fueled the boom more than any aesthetic strivings) in which art values skyrocketed. In 1987, the stock market crashed. By 1991, most of the Soho art galleries had been converted to furniture stores. Art was dead.

But of course it wasn't. Instead of dying, the art community became more lively, more organically charged. Artists and dealers who had previously been excluded from the galaxy of elite galleries found themselves given an opportunity to remake the face of art and how it was sold; how it was delivered to the masses. The "Do-It-Yourself" (D.I.Y.) art movement was born. Unable to establish and maintain museum-like galleries filled with rare talent and rare air, D.I.Y. dealers changed the rules. They held shows in rented hotel rooms, or in their own apartments. Rather than recreating the toffee-nosed atmosphere of tony galleries, they revived the practice of the intimate salon, bringing artists and buyers together for a meal. Some artists forsook the dealer route completely, mounting shows of their own work—a practice dating back to the days when the Impressionists grew tired of waiting to be discovered and staged their own exhibition. It was a time for new thinking; a time for risk.

Writers today face a similar environment. Home computers, the Internet, the Web, CD-ROM, all of these things have given rise to much speculation about the death of the written word. Anticipatory bouts of mourning the book have been going on for some time now. But what has really happened?

What has really happened is that writing, even—*gasp!*—the creation and maintenance of literature, has been turned over by default to a large segment of the masses. As we become more isolated and more equipped, markets for literature become necessarily more specifically defined. No longer can a few large publishers, in combination with a few prominent university professors and in consort with a few chosen writers, continue to define the literary canon. For many, including me, this is naturally unsettling and disorienting. But in fairness to a multicultural society, it is long overdue. And if you want to be a writer, it should be viewed in terms of possibility.

I often wish I was a writer in the time of Steinbeck and Hemingway. Back when a writer could write well and at length about important things and release work at regular intervals to a public hungry to read a book. Back when a novel had the potential to sustain a societal impact beyond the time the film version went to video. But this is a simplistic yearning that fails to take into account the obstacles earlier writers faced. It also fails to recognize the possibilities of today. Certainly, great change is underway in the literary world, and as are the roles of so many in a technological society, the role of the writer is changing. Gone are the days when a dose of angst and a cup of tea were enough—as if they ever were. But words—a writer's very substance—are still much in demand. They are simply required for different purposes, and in different arrangements. And this is where the New York art scene becomes instructive.

When the New York art world came crashing down around its Guccis, artists were faced with the collapse of a paradigm. Normal routes of accession and ascension were gone. There were new rules and new players. Artists had to find new ways to promote their work. And they did. The New York D.I.Y. art scene is working its way into the mainstream. Artists from the movement are being shown in the sleek galleries that remain from the boom days. The people who show up at these shows include the perennial monied aesthetes; they also include skateboarders. The end result? A movement that has infused the snooty prestige of the old with the energy of the new. The caste system has been disrupted. Much the same is true for writers today.

The market for writing is fluid, plastic. Always changing. But while all around you is changing, keep this in mind. Whether they show up on a bound page, on a radio wave, or on a screen, words must first be composed by a writer. Adopt the D.I.Y. mentality, and you'll be just fine.

## WHERE DO I GO TO DO IT MYSELF?

As I said in the previous section, wherever you see words, someone wrote them. And in many cases, when you *hear* words, someone wrote them. My main focus is writing for magazines. But rare is the writer who can survive on writing for magazines alone. As do many freelancers, I have supplemented my magazine writing income with commercial writing of all sorts, and continue to do so. Each writer must decide which mix of writing to pursue. Some freelancers perform commercial writing exclusively, and quite frankly, if you have the right skills and personality, that's where the money is. Robert W. Bly's *Secrets of a Freelance Writer* is an excellent source of seed ideas for freelancers interested in commercial outlets for their writing.

Bly's way is not my way, however. He states that he spends ninety-five percent of his time taking care of work for corporate clients; I've been there, and now I have chosen (and have the luxury) to pursue a different balance of profit versus personal fulfillment. My focus has always been, and continues to be, on nonfiction journalism, essays, and humor. I am not interested in pushing my commercial writing skills as aggressively as Bly recommends. This is not intended to be dismissive. It simply reflects a different focus. Bly loves his work, finds it fulfilling, he's good at it, and he earns a six-figure income. I love my work, I find it fulfilling, I keep learning, and my income is nowhere near six figures. But we both make a living writing. And it's no accident that I own a copy of Bly's book—many of his tips got me work in the early days, and I recommend them to you.

In the chapters to follow, I have divided writing into two categories: commercial writing and writing for publication. "Writing for publication" is a broad designation and, as a result, inexact. I considered using the term "magazine writing," but it is limiting. I considered the term "journalism," but that too fails to adequately address the category. To further confuse the point, magazine writing is ultimately sponsored by advertisers, and can therefore feasibly be extrapolated to be commercial writing; so the designation "noncommercial writing" seems inappropriate. In the end, I have settled on "writing for publication" because it reflects a process that is more primarily writer-driven than client-driven.

The chapter on commercial writing is intended as an overview; the rest of the book focuses on writing for publication. I have done my share of commercial writing, and will share what I know. However, there are a number of resources written by full-time commercial writers that will nicely serve your needs should you choose to concentrate your efforts in that area. My goal is simply to make you aware of the possibilities, give you a few tips and directions, and then, for the rest of the book, focus my efforts on writing for publication, as that has emerged as my area of emphasis.

# CHAPTER FOUR

# COMMERCIAL WRITING

Honesty prevents me from saying that the feeling I get when a television spot I've written airs is the same as that I get when I see one of my essays in print. It isn't. For some people it would be, and that, I guess, is determined by the individual. But I still approach commercial work with two things in mind: My client expects and deserves my finest, most focused effort (see sidebar, "Keep Your Heart In It"), and throughout each project, I'm developing my writing skills.

In *Secrets of a Freelance Writer,* Bob Bly writes, "there can be great joy, dignity, and pride in being a successful commercial writer." With the caveat that I detest *false* pride, I agree. The creative process remains the creative process whether you are developing the denouement of an introspective essay or the tagline for a punchy radio commercial.

I relish wrestling with a concept, working to convert words to messages, messages to words. I enjoy immersing myself in a surplus of information, sifting through it all, searching for the elements that eventually coalesce to suggest a unifying theme. And whether I'm working on thirty seconds' worth of radio copy, a print ad, or a billboard, I still get that thrill at the point of breakthrough: that point when the first idea suggests itself, and is then followed by a torrent of possibilities.

Next comes the tough work of winnowing the "torrent of possibilities" down to a lean, focused piece of work that best serves the interest of your client. Depending on the type of work and the type of client, the nature of your work may be highly processed. While this may seem artistically limiting, it is a reality that you can turn to your advantage. Just as poets develop their craft by working within the constraints of form (eschewing free verse to fulfill the requirements of the villanelle, for example), so too can you develop new abilities and perspectives as a writer by applying your talents within the constraints of a corporate directive. The person who can be creative without constraint is doing the expected; the person who finds a way to be creative within parameters of control is developing skills valuable to clients and valuable to the writer.

Any writer hoping to have an impact on the reader must learn to write with that reader in mind. The lessons commercial writing provide in this respect are invaluable. By its very nature, commercial writing is audience driven. From corporate reports to direct mail, audience reaction and response is of paramount concern. Every time you choose a word, you must weigh its use to you as a writer against its power to attract and maintain the interest of the reader. You must learn to write using your hand, but an imaginary listener's ears. As you hone this sensibility, your commercial work will become more and more effective and audience appropriate. And as these lessons translate to your noncommercial work (and they will), your work will become more powerful; the reader will feel its impact at a more personal level.

## The Artist Speaks: Isn't Commercial Writing a Sell-Out?

Um, yes, with any luck at all, commercial writing is a sell-out. But commercial writing does so much more than pay the rent. I've learned much from commercial writing that has strengthened my noncommercial writing. Consider, for instance, radio copy.

When a friend of mine started an advertising agency and hired me to write radio copy, I had a tough time. I was used to meeting word counts, but I had never been forced to write within the dictates of time—let alone complete a coherent thought in the space of thirty seconds! My partner had been doing it for nearly twenty-five years. Even though I was considered "the writer," and he the "radio guy," he has taught me invaluable writing lessons through his editing of my radio copy. From him I have learned the power of leanness, directness, the beauty of the ellipsis. And now these things show up in the rhythms of my writing every day.

A writer composing copy for a television spot must consider how the words will be colored by what the viewer sees on the screen. Will the images stand in contrast? Will the images reinforce the words, or *vice versa*? Will the viewer ignore the words and attend only to the images? The lessons learned from these considerations cause the writer to reexamine words for the substance of their sounds as well as their meaning.

Any commercial writer who has ever composed a print ad has given consideration to the value of "white space." Is it any stretch of the imagination then, for me to suggest that the study of such composition will somehow inform the poet who contemplates the shape of a work upon the page?

Above all, commercial writing serves to broaden your experience, and experience, as we discussed in Chapter Two, is what makes a writer.

One of the things I enjoy about my "noncommercial" work is the wide range of unique individuals I meet. Commercial writing provides an equally interesting opportunity to meet a wide range of individuals and explore topics you were unaware of a week ago. Commercial assignments have put me in contact with fascinating individuals and cutting-edge technology. Commercial assignments have delivered me to soundstages and state-of-the-art digital editing suites. Commercial assignments frequently arm me with material for essays and extended nonfiction pieces. By their very nature, commercial assignments keep you current.

Commercial writing has supported my writing habit to varying degrees since the day I first left the regular workforce, and it continues to do so. Commercial writing continues to present me with new challenges and new opportunities, and the projects I work on are consistently interesting. In the end, the thing I value most about commercial writing is the thing I value most, period: *writing.*

## HOW MUCH COMMERCIAL WRITING SHOULD I DO?

The answer to the question of how much commercial writing to do comes in two parts: As much as it takes, and as much as you like.

In my case, "as much as it takes," has varied over the years. For the first two years of my writing career, I took a day job that involved a form of commercial writing. I began by proofreading brochures for legal seminars and writing bios for seminar faculty. (May I digress for a moment to point out that you haven't journeyed to the farthest corners of fatuous prose until you've edited a self-penned bio by an attorney doing a half-day seminar on estate planning and probate. If you think *artistes* are notorious for the delicate nature of their egos, try suggesting to a middle-aged probate attorney in Fargo that due to space constraints you're going to exclude reference to his victorious captainship of the college mock trial team back in '68.) The pay was mild, but it was regular work, and it was work with words. I minded my p's and q's on the proofreading front, held my own in the bio department, and soon I was given the opportunity to write program summaries. This was interesting, as I was called upon to summarize the content of a seminar I would never attend on a topic I would never understand for an audience I would never meet. It is no coincidence that the ability to perform all three of these functions bode well for my future as a full-time freelancer.

## Keep Your Heart in It

Although I view commercial writing as a way to supplement income earned by writing that is closer to my soul, I do not approach commercial projects at half throttle. Make no mistake: if you treat commercial writing assignments strictly as a means to an end, your means will quickly come to an end. Your commercial clients expect and deserve professional attention, and will quickly detect anything less.

By harboring disrespect for commercial assignments you will also cheat yourself as a writer. I cannot recall a commercial assignment that didn't require me to engage in the creative process just as if I were working on an essay, or the lead to a piece of nonfiction. Why short-circuit that process? Remember, even if you don't desire a career as a commercial freelancer, this is the place to get those "chops" we talked about in Chapter One. At its most basic level, writing is writing. With apologies to Nike (and the reader), learning to *just do it* is critical, whether you're writing a piece of direct mail or an essay examining the '90s as a period of declension in the world of modern art.

Throughout my stint as a proofreader, I continued to ask my supervisor for more work involving actual writing. One of the tasks she assigned forced me to develop both my vocabulary and persuasive writing techniques. When an unreasonable customer had exhausted the considerable patience of our customer service department (and they were considerably patient; I used to sit adjacent and marvel at the vitriol ricocheting out of their headsets), it fell to me to compose a letter designed to resolve the matter. In general, these letters began with a nutshell description of our understanding of the situation, moved on to review our policies as they applied to the circumstance in question, and then detailed the customer's options. These were not form letters; I composed each personally only after reviewing all previous correspondence with the customer, reviewing the brochure promoting the seminar in question, speaking with the customer service representative involved, and, if necessary, any on-site seminar staff involved. In a letter, I would then explain the finer points of the fine print, explicate company policy regarding failure to observe the rules of advance cancellation notification, and generally spend a paragraph or two establishing the fact that no, despite the fact that you are an attorney, you are angry, and you have slung a number of large words our way, you can't bully us into compromising our position. All in terms as delicate as they were firm. And of course, each letter closed with a peace offering. Surprisingly, this offer was accepted on a fairly regular basis, and I became popular with the folks in customer service, because, as so many writers have heard, I "had a way with words." I was also given a wider range of writing and research assignments. By the time I was ready to leave the job to freelance full time, I was spending the bulk of my time at the company completing projects assigned to me by virtue of my eagerness to do anything that involved writing.

And of course, by night, lunch hour, and the occasional afternoon off, I was developing my freelance career. Just over two years after I began proofreading brochures, I was ready to take the full-time freelance plunge, and I've been freelance ever since. But for every essay I've published, there have been any number of car sales promoted, brochures written, and CEO letters edited. Finding commercial work is critical to the freelancer's survival.

But what is it, and where do you find it?

## WHAT NEEDS TO BE WRITTEN?

Commercial writing fills a spectrum ranging from brochures to business plans, from advertisements to audiovisuals. As I look around my office, I see commercial writing everywhere:

- A bumper sticker, designed and written for a radio station
- The liner notes for a CD box set of collected music
- A mailer announcing the release of the 1996 North American Emergency Response Guidebook
- The owner's manual for my computer
- "Closed" and "Open" placards with slogans designed and written for a pizza company
- A concert poster
- A hospital newsletter
- A videotape containing a series of television commercials.
- A piece of direct mail from *Writer's Digest*
- *The View,* a quarterly publication from my alma mater
- A mail-order catalog filled with cheery blurbs touting each product
- The prospectus for a mutual fund

I made that list in under two minutes, without leaving my chair, reading the business section of the local newspaper, picking up the phone, or heading out on the Internet. In the next two minutes, I can think of several other types of commercial writing assignments I've been involved in personally:

- Regional vacation guides
- Regional restaurant guides
- Annual reports
- Chamber of Commerce publications
- Brochures
- Point-of-purchase displays (anything you see promoting a product where it's sold—grocery store displays, for instance)
- Press releases

- Radio commercials
- Newsletters
- Corporate speeches
- Scripts for press conferences
- Trade show display panels
- Billboards
- Television commercials
- Promotional copy
- Corporate resumes
- Product descriptions
- Corporate profiles

Enough. The point is, wherever you see or hear writing appearing on behalf of a commercial establishment, someone was paid to write it. "Someone" may have been an hourly employee who usually proofreads brochures, or a highly paid freelancer. Whether they realize it or not, virtually every company in existence employs commercial writers. Your key to success is to convince them to employ you.

## FINDING COMMERCIAL CLIENTS

Pardon my psychobabble, but before you can find commercial clients, you have to find yourself. You must identify your strengths and establish areas of focus. Will you specialize, or work as a generalist? What special qualities, knowledge, skills do you possess that make you of purchasable worth to any particular commercial client?

As I mentioned previously, I'm a registered nurse. To illustrate my point about "finding yourself," please allow me to expand on the comments I made in Chapter Two. Although I last worked as a nurse in 1989, I have maintained my license, and still have a general familiarity with the status of the nursing profession and health care in general. This background has proven valuable to me in obtaining commercial assignments—indeed, two of my most sustaining clients were obtained as a direct result of my health care background. One is a hospital. Several times a year they ask me to contribute pieces to the hospital magazine they mass mail. They are interested in hiring someone who can write an interesting, accurate story, but they also value the fact that I have a working understanding of the techniques and terminology I may encounter while researching the piece. They also trust that I will translate these things to terms lay readers will understand.

The other client is a medical publisher, for which I compose chapters of medical/legal textbooks. Again, it is the combination of my nursing and writing backgrounds that led me to query the company, and it is that same combination that has resulted in them sending me a steady diet of work.

Beyond those two consistent clients, my nursing background has proven unexpectedly beneficial in obtaining and developing a number of commercial projects. I have helped professors at the university school of nursing develop critical papers and articles for publication in professional journals. I have assisted a graduate nurse in the development of her master's thesis. When I was involved in writing and directing a series of commercials for a regional cancer center, my experience working with a nursing colleague who has written extensively on the subject of breast cancer proved invaluable. I went back to my notes from that project and reread transcripts of women describing their cancer experiences. Informed by the voices of these women, the copy for the commercials rang true. I didn't have to "make up" the words a woman might use to express how she felt when she learned she had cancer; I had already heard those words spoken by the numerous women who participated in the study I helped my colleague write.

## Should I Work Big or Small?

Most of the commercial writing I have done has been for small to mid-size corporations. Smaller companies have smaller budgets and generally produce a limited number of projects. On the other hand, you are more likely to deal directly with the folks at the top. If you do good work, your relationship with the company will be personal and personable.

At larger corporations, you might find yourself working on a project with someone two or three levels removed from the origin of the project. Approval times may be extended while your project wends its way through hierarchical channels. However, larger companies are likely to have larger budgets, and provide more regular opportunities for freelancers.

Examine your own interests. Are there subjects with which you have greater familiarity than the average Joe or Jane? If so, chances are you can parlay that familiarity into writing work. Are you like me, a writer who has a degree in something other than writing? Pursue writing assignments in the area of your training.

Beyond interests or training, examine your employment history. Has your work brought you in contact with knowledge valuable to commercial clients? When a friend and I submitted a marketing campaign proposal to a professional organization of physical therapists, my experience working as a physical therapy aide and rehabilitation nurse (coupled with my friend's creativity and salesmanship) won us the account.

Generalist or specialist, you still have to get started. Here are a few ways to find commercial work:

**Pay Attention (Surprise!).** How are local businesses advertising their services? Television? Radio? Newspaper? Brochures? Direct mail? Can you help them do a better job? If so, perhaps it's time to introduce yourself.

**Knock on Doors.** Spend time perusing the telephone business directory or Yellow Pages. Look for companies large enough to generate corporate reports, companies you are uniquely suited to assist. Make an appointment to discuss your services. The in-person meeting is best; take a phone conversation if that's all you can get. But always follow up with written correspondence that makes direct reference to the meeting.

**Be Prepared.** It's not enough to knock on doors and then say "What do you need?" Research the business you'll be meeting with. Assess their likely needs. Identify specific areas in which you can be of assistance. Familiarity with a company is functionally essential; it is also flattering to the individual you will be meeting with.

**Listen.** As important as it is to prepare a pitch, it is equally important to listen to what a potential client is telling you. I'm oversimplifying, but if you get so caught up in pitching your proposal for a fully illuminated brochure that plays *Ode to Joy* upon opening, you may miss the client's mentioning his need for a forty-page manual on the proper care and packaging of sugar beets. One is your idea of what the company needs; the other is paying work.

**Remain Ever Vigilant.** You never know when a chance encounter will turn into work. I've obtained more than one assignment when I mentioned in conversation that I was a freelance writer. Your timing must be right, and you mustn't become a crashing bore about the whole thing, but it doesn't hurt to work it into conversation.

**Don't Leave Home Without It.** Get a set of business cards and carry them with you wherever you go. Hand them out whenever you get the chance. And always remember the most important rule of business cards: Whenever possible, *exchange* them. The odds of someone calling you to follow up on an informal conversation are generally small. But by making that call yourself, you demonstrate that you are attentive, professional, and serious in your desire to work.

**Follow Up.** Whenever you make a contact, whether that contact has work for you or not, follow up with a letter. Remain brief, professional, and polite; that's the impression you want to make. Make an identifiable reference to the conversation or meeting in question, thank the individual for the opportunity to speak, and if you were given an assignment, thank the individual and then get to work on it. If the meeting didn't produce any work for you, make it known that you continue to be interested in any future work that might arise—and then prove it by following up at regular, polite intervals.

**Word of Mouth.** Once you get the ball rolling, you'll discover that word of mouth is everything you've heard it to be. Just remember: word of mouth cuts both ways.

**Set Limits.** At some point, you will have to learn to say no. The client may be offering too little money; the work might be too specialized, too general, or completely beyond your scope of expertise; you may have too much other work. If this seems self-defeating, just contrast the client who receives a polite, explanatory "no" to the client who receives an ill-advised "yes" only to have the whole job disintegrate into a mass of recriminations, poor quality, and missed deadlines.

## HOW TO KEEP THE BALL ROLLING

"Leads" in the writing world are often tangential and interconnected, and commercial writing leads are no different. Once you get that first assignment and execute it professionally, it is likely it will lead to others. But the process is not passive; you must think actively, and use yourself and your skills as a catalyst for more work. There are a number of ways you can keep the commercial pot boiling:

**Follow Up, Follow Through.** When you've completed an assignment for a client, send a letter of thanks. Tell the client you're interested in any additional work he or she might provide. Close by saying you'll call in a week to follow up. This allows the client time to identify projects for which you might be of use. Then, in a week, make that call. You'll be surprised at how much work you can generate with this simple, straightforward process.

**Touch Base.** It sounds like biz-speak: "Hi, Fred, I'm just touching base." But if you're sincere, a well-timed call to a client you haven't worked with for a while is a valuable way to keep your name in the mix, move it up the list. Calling every other day is being a pest; calling at just the right time is profitable.

**Watch for Developments That Affect Your Clients.** If changes in the business world affect your client, chances are there's work to be done, and you can do it. And if you bring something to the attention of clients before they notice it, you'll demonstrate both your attentiveness and your commitment.

**Watch for Related Clients.** Whether you begin as a specialist or develop into one, you'll generate a certain amount of commercial work through clients who share similarities. Any time you can streamline your work by including work or experience already established, you increase your profit. So keep an eye out for clients with needs similar to those you already serve. Of course, there are a few common-sense rules of engagement that must be observed if you wish to avoid shooting yourself in the foot. You must be aboveboard. You mustn't compromise a client's confidentiality. You mustn't resell previously owned work. And you shouldn't expect to keep a client happy while churning out work for a competitor.

**Come Right Out and Ask.** Ask your clients if they know of anyone else who might need your services. Not only is it likely they can recommend clients to you, they can recommend you to clients. A built-in reference never hurts.

**Pay Attention.** Pay attention to all the things that got you work in the first place.

### PROMOTING YOURSELF

"Promoting yourself" sounds pretty distasteful. But if people don't know you, they don't hire you.

Beyond business cards, the occasional letter, numerous phone calls, and the delivery of acceptable work, I haven't had to engage in a lot of active promotion. But if you intend to develop your commercial writing beyond the level of a sideline occupation, you'll need to promote your work. You can accomplish this through obvious means (print ads, brochures, direct mail) or less-obvious means (public speaking, publishing a newsletter). Robert Bly's *Secrets of a Freelance Writer* contains an entire chapter devoted to marketing your freelance services. I've dipped into it over the years and recommend it wholeheartedly.

Never forget: The number-one device of self-promotion, the one that will get you more work than any brochure, sales pitch, or marketing scheme, is *quality work.*

## HOW MUCH SHOULD I CHARGE?

Most books addressing commercial writing have a section titled "How Much Should I Charge?" Mine has one too. But mine contains no numbers. No dollar signs. Because most of those same books end up providing a "range" figure, which means you'll have to figure it out on your own anyway. And it's tough. Putting a price on the generally intangible always has been. No way around it, in the beginning you'll have to feel your way around this issue. What I can do is provide you with some guidelines.

How much you charge depends on a number of factors:

- *Your status.* Are you a beginner, or are you established? You may have to underprice yourself to gain a toehold, but don't dig a hole from which you can't crawl out.
- *The client.* What is the budget for this project? What has the client paid in the past for similar work?
- *The competition.* What is the competition charging? Is it worth your while to undercut them, or would you prefer to prove your greater worth by providing better-quality service? And here's a sneaky way to find out what the competition is charging: Ask them! Most will tell you.
- *Your landlord.* Is the rent overdue, with no work in sight? You may have to adjust your rates downward to generate some quick cash.
- *Your workload.* If you've got more work than you can handle, you've got a good hand of cards to play. Now's the time to bump your rates, or politely turn down less profitable projects. Just don't fill the air with the smell of burning bridges.
- *The nature of the project.* Do you bring a special expertise to the table that makes you more qualified to do the work than the competition? Is that expertise worth money to the client? Can you prove it?

One way to increase your income is to develop an area or two of specialty. Specialists generally make more money and have more regular work.

## GETTING PAID

Before you take on any project, work out the terms of your agreement in advance and put them in writing. On large projects, it is not unreasonable and not unwise to ask for a portion of the payment in advance.

If you agree to work by the hour, keep these things in mind:

- Is there a limit on how long the project will take?
- Will meetings, travel, and phone time be billed at the same hourly rate?

If you are being paid by the project, consider these items:

- Does your fee include revisions? If so, is there a limit to those revisions?
- Are allowances built in for unforeseen developments, such as the need to do additional research?

For all projects, regardless of the nature of the payment schedule, establish the following:

- What is the level of client control over your work?
- What will happen if the client is displeased with the finished product?
- Which expenses are you expected to absorb, and which will be reimbursed by the client?

Whatever your terms are, establish them clearly from the "get-go." Put things in writing. This is not suspicious behavior; it is professional behavior.

## *NOT* GETTING PAID

I've been fortunate. In general, I've been paid what I was promised. I was stiffed once: The client and I had an agreement in writing, and I held up my end; his end was to write me a check for $800, but it never happened. As it was, about the time I finished the job, I learned that the individual in question had run into—I'll frame this delicately—a touch of misfortune on both the personal and professional fronts. I made a few relatively weak attempts to collect. When I read in the business section of a local paper that he was being sued by a few other businesses for unpaid bills with several more zeros to the left of the decimal than mine, I decided to treat the experience as an $800 business seminar filled with a number of useful lessons and let it go.

It was a relatively small town. I wasn't going hungry. He had plenty of trouble as it was. Perhaps some day he'll surprise me with a check. In the meantime, I moved on.

But what are your collection options? Well, begin with a pleasant reminder. If a month has passed and you haven't received payment, send a second copy of the bill, accompanied by a polite reminder. A digression: As someone who was once responsible for paying a large number of bills for a small advertising agency, I detested cutesy reminders. The sad-face stamp that read, "Have you forgotten us?" or the cartoony crustacean sticker that read, "I don't mean to be *crabby* . . . " tended to trigger the worst in me. An additional two-week passive/aggressive delay in payment often ensued.

So. Simply make a polite, straightforward request for payment.

If two more weeks pass without payment, it's time to make a phone call. Some sources recommend a tougher letter, followed by a third invoice including a late-payment charge in the form of interest calculated on a thirty-day cycle. I recommend a phone call. If you're being fobbed off, nasty letters and threats of additional fees may do the trick, but it's unlikely. Make a phone call, and speak directly to the person in charge of paying invoices. State your case politely and firmly. If you're told the check is in the mail or will be soon, get specifics. If the check doesn't show when it should, get back on the phone.

In *Secrets of a Freelance Writer,* Bob Bly recommends that all correspondence sent after the first "reminder" letter be sent certified mail, return receipt requested. This method not only lets you know the message arrived, it rates a little higher on the conscience-pricking meter.

And if you *still* don't get paid? If you feel the amount is substantial, you might retain the services of a professional collector or attorney, but in some cases, the amount you're after won't support that sort of endeavor. Small claims court is also an option; the amount you're seeking will have to meet the minimum standard set by your state. The bottom line? As a one-person business, your collection powers are limited.

Don't overlook the possibilities of negotiation. You may be able to arrange payment over time, or payment at a reduced rate. Obviously, this isn't the optimum result, but it's better than ineffectual threats. It's better than a long, drawn-out feud that nets nothing. I was once involved in a situation with a nonpaying client besieged with legal attempts to drain blood from the client's exsanguinated turnip. While the lawsuits and collection notices flew thick and fast, my partner quietly sat down with the client, recognized the client's predicament, and indicated our willingness to work something out. Every once in a while, my partner dropped in to politely reinforce our sincere and continued interest in receiving payment, and every once in a while over the next year, a partial payment showed up in the mail. By the end of the year, we had been paid in full. The other creditors were still slinging legalese, and were still unpaid.

A note: Many commercial clients make a regular practice of paying bills on a sixty- or ninety-day cycle. Screaming down the telephone thirty-one days after you mail your invoice is unlikely to change this policy.

## IN A NUTSHELL

Commercial writing will be what you want it to be: a supportive sideline, or a fulfilling career. As is so often so true, the basics are what it's all about: Follow through, be good to your word, get paid what you're worth, return your phone calls.

Spell right, be neat.

CHAPTER FIVE

# WRITING FOR PUBLICATION

From here on, we'll be focusing on writing most likely to end up in magazines. Magazines reflect the society they serve: As you might expect, the American magazine scene is fantastically diverse and in a constant state of flux.

Magazines have always come and gone, and they continue to come and go by the hundreds each year, but the past few years have been record-breakers. The periodical rack at your local bookstore groans beneath the weight of an explosion of magazines. Many of the venerable old standards still soldier on, but they are fighting for space amongst a multitude of upstarts.

## THE MAGAZINE EXPLOSION

Why all the activity? Well, computers have certainly done their part. For one thing, they've spawned an entire magazine genre of their own. But more to the point, advances in desktop publishing have opened magazine publishing to an entirely new group of people. Twenty minutes in an electronics superstore and you can pick up all the equipment you need to produce the prepress version of your own full-blown magazine.

Another element of the profusion has to do with publishers' aggressive development of "niche" markets by tailoring content to a very specific audience. Rare is the magazine intended to address the nation as a whole; it is far more likely that a magazine will address you specifically, as a fan of Midwestern country living, haiku, or professional wrestling.

Finally, this is the Age of Information. Information is accruing at an exponential rate, and it can be gathered, shaped, and shipped like never before. And while the Information Age is most closely associated with the rise of electronic media, far from going the way of the stone tablet, the magazine industry has become energized. Say what you will about the growth of electronic publishing, it is yet in its gurgling infancy, and you still can't beat the portability and user-friendliness of a magazine. At this point, most electronic publications exist to *augment,* rather than replace, the printed version. Laptops aside, if you will, it's still tough to take a Webzine aboard the train or into the bathroom.

Strangely enough, despite the fact that many folks felt electronic technology would be the death of paper magazines, it has turned out recently that *paper* has been the death of many magazines. Paper costs have been climbing steadily and quickly over the past few years, and the trend is prognosticated to continue. Mailing costs have also increased. Tax code changes have affected costs of print production. The result? Higher subscription prices and space reductions (as in less words to be written and paid for) in some cases, termination of the publication in other cases.

And so what does all this mean to you as a freelancer? For one thing, amidst all this turmoil, change, and uncertainty, one thing remains constant, no matter what form—print or electronic—the magazine takes over the next decade, no matter how many magazines start up or fold, no matter how narrow the niches get, good writing will continue to be in demand. It is up to you to pay attention and do good work, but in the end, it all comes down to writing. To you and the words.

## FOR WHOM SHOULD I WRITE?

As a writer, the magazine explosion means one thing: You have more markets for your writing than ever before. So how do you decide where to focus your efforts? There are a number of ways to break down the possibilities.

### Old versus New

As a general rule, established magazines pay better than start-ups, and an established publication is more likely to stay around long enough for your check to clear.

Not all start-ups start up on a shoestring, however. John F. Kennedy, Jr., launched the "political lifestyle" magazine *George* with substantial financial backing; in a genre where shoestring start-ups are nearly *de rigueur,* the literary magazine *DoubleTake* hit the stands armed with a substantial grant and has since received an even larger endowment. A little research, a little experience, and you'll soon develop a sense of the future in store for a new magazine.

New magazines are frequently a good place to get your foot in. In some cases they seek the services of new writers because they can't afford established writers. In other cases, by virtue of their newness or narrowly focused content, there may be no established writers in the genre.

You can spot new magazine start-ups by monitoring the trade journals. Publications like *Writer's Digest, Successful Freelancing,* and *Editor & Writer* (see Resources in Chapter Sixteen) regularly announce the launch of new periodicals; in many cases, they report the rumblings of such news well in advance of the actual event, giving you time to do a little research and form a plan of attack. But act quickly: you'll never have a better opportunity to get in on the ground floor, and you can bet a legion of other writers will make the same move.

It is generally much more difficult to break in at an established magazine than at a start-up, but don't be discouraged. The hard work is worth the rewards: better pay, better clips, and less likelihood that your carefully cultivated connection will disappear overnight. When the struggle gets frustrating, remember that regardless of who you are or aren't, editors are interested in timely topics and excellent writing. Hone your eye for the first and your talent for the second, toss in a hefty dose of don't-quit, and you'll be fine.

## Love or Money?

For the full-time freelancer, the choice is basic: paying gigs are a necessity, and the whole process of pitching articles is driven by the ability to turn writing into rent. Writing for high fulfillment and low pay is a luxury. But it's a luxury with benefits.

When I'm pitching a story idea, I begin by creating a list of magazines for which the topic is appropriate. I then order that list based on one mercenary principle: who pays the most! Then I work my way down from the top, submitting proposals to high-paying markets first.

But I've done—and continue to do—plenty of writing in which remuneration ranges from minuscule to missing.

Sometimes I do this with an eye to the future. If you spot a fledgling publication with potential, your early contributions may be a form of investment—not necessarily commanding top dollar at the outset, but potentially rewarding in the long term, should the magazine thrive.

Sometimes I write for low or no pay simply for the opportunity to write recreationally, or to address a topic that moves me more than it does an editor's pocketbook. Most freelancers—including me—cite a love for writing over compensation as the driving motivation behind their career choice. Sometimes you get a chance to prove it!

An example from my recent writing past serves to illustrate the point. Since the time I first heard a Waylon Jennings eight-track in the cab of a four-wheel-drive pickup when I was a teenager working on a ranch in Wyoming, I've developed an interest in country music; a genre that up until that time gave me all the pleasure of amateur dental work. Over the years, I've maintained a passing acquaintance with the state of country, and most recently have bemoaned its transformation into superficial pop music sung largely by individuals who hadn't worn a cowboy hat until their A&R people wedged one on their heads. In my humble opinion, true country artists were being lost in a haze of dry-ice smoke and obscured by line-danceable laser shows. Then a friend gave me a copy of a brand-new magazine by the name of *No Depression*. Evolved from a music message board on America Online, the first issue was thin and humble. But I loved the editorial "take." The artist profiles and reviews concentrated on the very music mainstream country radio stations were giving such short shrift. And so I contacted the editor. In the third issue, I contributed a concert review and an album review. I've had a little something in each issue since then. Initially, the magazine paid nothing. Recently, they've grown, and begun to pay—albeit very modestly—for some of their material.

Am I selling my services too cheaply? Based on other sales, yes. But based on the fact that this is a young, growing magazine, I'm willing to invest some time with them. And based on the fact that the editor allows me wide creative latitude to write about a topic of personal interest, I think I'm taking advantage of an opportunity to develop a whole new area of expertise.

And dang it, it's fun!

Of course, early in your freelance career, you may write for low pay not out of love, but of necessity; to garner publication credits, to learn the ropes, to establish a niche.

## Consumer Magazines

Most of the magazines you'll find on newsstands or in bookstores are consumer magazines—high-profile publications intended for popular consumption. For freelancers, the consumer magazine market represents a kaleidoscopic array of opportunity. The *1997 Writer's Market* consumer magazine directory features 70 categories of consumer magazines, ranging from "Animal" to "Women's." In between, you'll find magazines categorized under "Astrology, Metaphysical and New Age," "Health and Fitness," "Retirement," "Relationships," and more.

Major consumer magazines pay handsomely, and deliver your writing to an audience that may reach into the tens of millions. Not-so-major consumer magazines pay little or nothing, and may deliver your writing to an audience in the tens of tens.

## Trade Magazines

Trade magazines (also known as business, technical, and professional journals) are targeted to a specific audience defined by profession. *Writer's Digest* is a trade magazine targeted to writers. *Bobbin* magazine is published for apparel and sewn products manufacturers. *911 Magazine* serves public safety communications and response personnel. *Aqua* bills itself as "The Business Magazine for Spa and Pool Professionals." From pencil pushers to pool peddlers, trade magazines epitomize the concept of niche readership.

Trade magazines have a relatively low profile in comparison to their consumer counterparts, and as a result, many freelancers overlook them. Take the time to seek them out, and you will discover a market where editors are accessible, pay is competitive with high-profile commercial publications, and regular work is . . . well . . . more *regular*.

Must you possess an intimate understanding of advertising theory in order to write for *Advertising Age*? Not necessarily. But you will find that your ability to write for some trades is limited if you don't know the business. Don't be shy—approach the editors and find out what they need in a writer. More often than not, they don't need an expert in their field, they need someone who can get the story, get it right, and get it in on time.

Another nice thing about writing for trade magazines, based on my experience, is that once an editor learns to like you, that editor is much more likely to come to *you* with ideas than are his or her consumer magazine counterparts.

Don't automatically assume that writing trade magazine copy is dry, just-the-facts business. Much of it is, but I've run into a couple of trade magazine editors who have given me more creative latitude than I've had for many a commercial magazine assignment. It's a mistake to assume you'll be churning out dry, technical copy.

It's also a mistake to think you'll spend your time reporting the price of yarn or interviewing corporate executives in stuffy offices. In truth, you never know where you'll end up. I recently did a piece for a trucking trade magazine for which I spent two days at training camp with the Chicago Bears. I got to have dinner in the players' dining room. The gastronomical visions I viewed I recall with wonder still.

## Watch Your Step!

When you write for trade magazines, be on your toes. You're writing for an audience that knows its stuff. Like most editors, trade editors are looking for good writing professionally delivered, so you don't necessarily have to be an expert in the field—although appropriate background experience is a plus. But you will have to do your research and double check your work even more carefully than if you were writing for a general audience. Make a misstep, and you'll hear about it.

The same is true of any "special interest" commercial magazine. Mention the Hank Williams hit "Lovesick Blues" (written by Emmett Miller) in an article for *No Depression* magazine, and someone will fire off a letter to the editor pointing out that it was actually written by Irving Mills and Cliff Friend. From *Archaeology* to *Premiere* to *Workbasket,* special-interest subscribers pride themselves on obscure knowledge; slip, and they'll get you.

## Literary Magazines

Most "lit mags" have the life expectancy of a snail stuck on a drag strip; payment is usually in the form of complimentary copies or an apology. There are exceptions, of course. You may assign each one to a finger of your hands; you will still have enough unoccupied digits to pound out a rousing set of "Chopsticks."

Breaking into print with a quality literary magazine is about as easy as breaking into song with the Metropolitan Opera Company. Breaking into print with a poor-quality literary magazine is as easy as licking a stamp.

So. The pay is poor, the standards are either prohibitive or nonexistent. Is there room in the freelance life for literary pursuit? It depends.

If you are driven by the desire to elevate the process of writing beyond the expedient recitation of information, then I recommend that you set some of your writing time aside for a little literary windmill tilting. This is the kind of writing that hones your edge, forces you to redirect your attention. These are the type of publications that encourage you to take a run at territory you've never seen. In the end, writing for literary publications will serve you two ways: It will reinvest your writing with emotion, and it will add life to your "everyday" writing.

## Newspapers

I still place the occasional piece with a newspaper, but newspapers use freelancers sparingly, and belt-tightening has reduced that use even further. One of the major metropolitan publications that took some of my early work no longer works with freelancers, and it is my understanding that this is generally reflective of the industry.

Because the area in which I live has become well known for its outdoor music festivals, and because I've chiseled out a niche as a small-potatoes music writer, I am retained by a local newspaper to cover a series of concerts each summer as a sort of reporter/critic. It's a nice arrangement for decent pay, but beyond that I rarely do any newspaper writing.

If you're just starting out, you may find that newspapers offer you a chance to generate some publication credits. In my early days, I was traveling to Billings, Montana. I happened to know that humorist Dave

Barry would be speaking in Billings during my stay, and my local newspaper had just premiered his column. I asked if they'd be interested in a report on Dave Barry "live," and they gave me the go-ahead. I filed the story (including one of the shortest interviews in journalism history) with the paper upon my return, and got a modest check and a nice off-beat story to add to my portfolio.

Small-town weeklies are much more receptive to freelance work, but don't expect much—if any—pay. Still, it's another way to assemble your portfolio.

Armed with a good topic, good timing, and good writing, you might sell a piece to a newspaper's opinion page, but the competition is stiff, and most of the space is reserved for big-name columnists.

## REALITY CHECK

When it comes to calling it like it is, I cherish Bob Bly's take in *Secrets of a Freelance Writer:* "the sad fact is, writing magazine articles and books doesn't pay very well." He is right. He is telling you the truth. But if you've made it this far into the book, I'm afraid you're hooked.

So let's move on, and find out if you're the person who will be the exception to Bob Bly's rule.

### GET BACK TO THE RACK

Whenever you come across a magazine rack, whether it be in your local grocery store, in one of those mega-bookstores, or at a truck stop, take some time to scan. Even the best writing trade magazines miss a release here and there, and as comprehensive as *Writer's Market* may be, its listings are incomplete. You'll be surprised at the titles you find on a magazine rack that you won't find listed in a writer's guide.

One more thing: unless you have a photographic memory, carry a small notebook and jot down titles, addresses, content summaries, and so on. Better yet, if your budget allows, purchase a copy for your files.

And keep an eye out for freebies. Many trade or special interest magazines, from in-flight magazines to chain music store magazines, are free for the taking.

## Getting Glossy-Eyed

There's nothing wrong with shooting for publication in the big glossies. But don't neglect smaller, more obscure magazines that may surprise you with decent pay and regular work, as opposed to a once-in-a-lifetime assignment at top pay. If you think you've got an idea that will convince *National Geographic* to send you to Madagascar, by all means, fire away. But don't overlook that nuts-and-bolts piece on taxi service for the elderly for which *Midwestern Aging Digest* will give you money and print your words.

# CHAPTER SIX

# What Should I Write About?

Depending on your circumstance, the question "What should I write about?" may be answered for you. A month before I wrote this paragraph, an editor sent me an e-mail that read, in part, "What do you know about monster trucks?" Next to nothing. But I had a feeling I was about to learn more. I wrote back saying I didn't know a lot about the trucks themselves, but thanks to my blue collar roots, I did know a lot about the people who paid money to see them. I got the assignment.

Given an afternoon to compose a list of article ideas, I can give you my solemn word that the term "monster truck" would not have appeared. The term "water tower," on the other hand, would have been high on the list, because I have a personal interest in water towers as Americana, and I had recently proposed an article on the topic to another editor. But not monster trucks.

In the end, I found myself in Indianapolis at an off-road jamboree, milling around in the mud with thousands of monster truck aficionados, taking notes for an assigned piece. That same month, I crawled to the top of the local water tower (with permission of the village board and in the company of the town maintenance man) to take notes toward the completion of a piece assigned as a result of my proposal. The two different stories serve to illustrate the point that what you write about depends on how your stories are generated. As a freelancer, your writing will likely fall into one of three categories: writing what you think will sell; writing what you are asked to write about; and writing what you want to write about.

## WRITING WHAT YOU THINK WILL SELL

If you want to break into freelancing, you need to find a market for your writing. That's a nice way of saying you need to find someone who will give you money for what you write. And when you are starting out, it is generally the case that you won't be able to rely on assignments; you'll need to come up with ideas on your own. The challenge is to come up with something worth purchasing.

What is worth purchasing? There are a number of ways to find out. Look at copies of the magazine you want to write for. What type of articles do they run? What is their style? What can you tell about the readership by what you read on their pages? Obtain a set of writer's guidelines from the magazine (a simple note to the editor, accompanied by a self-addressed, stamped envelope is all it takes—and some writer's guidelines are available via e-mail). Writer's guidelines provide specific details about the type of material the magazine is interested in, including information on topics, style, and length. *Writer's Market* listings include information similar to writer's guidelines, and are helpful during your preliminary research, but they are no substitute for guidelines direct from the magazine itself. (See Chapter Seven for more information on writer's guidelines.)

Watch, read, and listen for information that suggests an article. Timeliness is critical to many publications, and if you can identify and anticipate a trend and tie it in with an idea for an article, you'll have a great chance of getting an editor's attention. Learn to look beyond the trend and anticipate its effect. Llama farming is on the increase in the United States? How will this affect sales of sheep's wool? Perhaps *Sheep! Magazine* or *National Lamb Wool Grower* will give you a chance to explore the topic.

Maintain a broad familiarity with the range of magazines in existence. When a bit of news or other information catches your eye, run it by your mental inventory of magazines to see if you come up with a potential match. Someone has invented a new bicycle seat? Biking magazines are an obvious choice, but they may already be on top of the story. Check with them, but expand your vision. Would *Popular Mechanics* be interested? Does a magazine exist that covers the fields of invention? If so, would they be interested in a profile of the inventor, or a small news piece on the new seat? What about the inventor himself? Is he over age 50? Perhaps *Modern Maturity* would be interested in a profile. Is he left-handed? Perhaps *Lefthander Magazine* would like a piece on his work. Is the inventor a woman? Perhaps it's time to review the Women's section of *Writer's Market.* Is the inventor an engineer and a member of a minority? Perhaps a query to *Minority Engineer* is in order.

See the possibilities? The salability of a story extends well beyond the obvious central topic. Think tangentially.

## WRITING WHAT YOU ARE ASKED TO WRITE ABOUT

As a general rule, you'll have to become established before editors approach you with assignments. And even if you do become established to this level with an editor or two, don't remain passive. Like any relationship, the editor/writer relationship requires attention and upkeep.

One way to increase your chances of being assigned work—even as a beginner—is to examine your areas of expertise, match them with specific publications, and then approach the editor as if you were applying for a job. Send a cover letter outlining your capabilities and qualifications uniquely matched to the publication in question. Accompany the letter with appropriate writing samples and a writing resume tailored to the publication's needs. If you fit the profile, an editor may give you an opportunity to complete an assigned piece. Treat the opportunity like the golden one it is, and you'll be rewarded with an ongoing source of assignments.

I enjoy "pitching" my own ideas, but I am equally happy to take on assigned pieces. In a sense, an assigned piece eliminates a large chunk of preliminary work. You can plunge right into a piece without wrestling with ways to sell it to an editor. It's already sold.

## WRITING WHAT YOU WANT TO WRITE ABOUT

Many of the ideas I pitch to editors revolve around topics that interest me personally. The primary reason for this is obvious, but there's more to it: I believe when you write about a topic that moves you personally, your writing will reflect your interest. The piece will be invested with a spark likely to be missing from a piece completed for strictly mercenary purposes.

## THE GREAT DEBATE: WRITE WHAT YOU KNOW? OR NO?

If you've done any reading at all about how to be a writer, you'll have come across the advice to "write what you know." In an interview published in the January 1996 edition of *Writer's Digest,* bestselling author Janet Dailey says, "The worst advice I ever got in my life was 'write what you know' . . . you can research and learn anything!"

When I set out to write a piece on monster trucks, I knew nothing about them. And so I researched. I obtained press kits from monster truck event promoters and one of the monster truck owners, looked at monster truck Web pages (yes, monster truck Web pages), read archived monster truck articles, brought up monster trucks in casual conversation (to find out what people didn't know, wanted to know, and preconceptions they held about monster trucks), and in the time leading up to completion of the article, generally kept my eyes and ears peeled for anything monster truck related. When I did the actual field research, spending three days with a monster truck crew during a national championship event, I asked even the most elementary questions: where they got the big tires, what fuel the trucks burned, why the accelerator pedal was so strangely shaped, etc. When it came time to write the piece, I was armed with all those critical bits of minutiae that can make the difference between a cursory overview-type article and a piece that truly takes the reader to the heart of the experience—whether it be monster truck racing or brain surgery.

Writing about something you don't "know" can help you avoid the pitfalls of assumption—of assuming your readers have any prior understanding of a subject. When you write about a topic with which you are very familiar, the danger always exists that you will assume your readership shares a similar knowledge base, or is at the very least familiar with the fundamentals. For instance, had I been an expert on monster truck racing, I might have failed to point out in my article that the sport no longer necessarily involves the crushing of cars, taking that bit of information for granted on behalf of myself and the reader. My readers might therefore have continued to assume (as I did, prior to doing the research for the piece) just the opposite.

As a writer, you are often serving as translator for the reader. If you are unfamiliar with the topic you are addressing, you will be less likely to fall into the trap of using esoteric jargon without explanation.

For example, when I was interviewing a lumberjack for an article on lumberjack competitions, I had to ask him what he meant when he referred to "birling." It turns out that "birling" means "log-rolling," and I was able to provide the translation to my readers. Had I been familiar with the term, I might have assumed my readership was as well.

In *1,082 Tips to Write Better and Sell More!*, a *Writer's Digest* special issue, Moira Anderson Allen provides another perspective on the value of writing what you don't know:

> An article written by "a leading authority" on a particular subject may be brilliant, but one-sided. Writers examine controversies from all sides, follow up leads and explore new angles by interviewing experts with differing opinions and experts in various fields.

Finally, writing about a topic with which you are unfamiliar can also lend a sense of discovery to your writing. If your writing reflects an active interest in a new subject, your readers will sense that interest. That doesn't mean you should write with wide-eyed wonder; but if you can make your reader feel as if he or she is discovering fascinating new territory at your side, your writing will take on a spirit of vitality readers will remember long after they've forgotten your flowery phrases. Perhaps this segment of the "write what you don't know" philosophy could be called the "write what you *want* to know" philosophy.

## But . . .

But what about all those articles that say you should write what you know?

Quoted in the same issue of *Writer's Digest* in which Janet Dailey made her comments, Kenneth Henson makes a case for writing what you know:

> Too often, writers ignore the common as they pursue the exotic and glamorous. Yet, it is our own personal experiences that we most understand. Our hobbies make good nonfiction articles, and each of us knows people who can become interesting and believable characters in our fiction.

From a practical standpoint, writing what you know can make things go faster. Research is less time-consuming, or may not be necessary at all. And while writing fueled by a sense of discovery is likely to be fresh and interesting, readers also love "inside information," and no one can share inside information like . . . well . . . an *insider.* Again, I quote Henson:

> Each of us is unique. This means that we maintain our residences, engage in hobbies, spend our vacations and perform our jobs a little differently than others. Because of your uniqueness, you perform some of your responsibilities better than most people. This means you have information that would help others. Analyze your own performance. Seek out those tasks you perform exceptionally well. These are topics you will enjoy writing about, and they are topics that will be easy for you.

The first article I ever had published (not the first article I ever *sold*—that's another story) was about the neurological rehabilitation unit on which I worked as a nurse. As in most areas of medicine, stunning advances have been made in the treatment of strokes, spinal cord injuries, and head injuries, and I came in contact with those advances daily. When I pitched the piece to a regional magazine, it didn't hurt that I was able to present credentials beyond the ability to write. The insider's viewpoint informs your perspective, allows you to share from a position of privity.

Beyond professional qualifications, your personal experience can lend impact to your writing. In addition to a familiarity with the technologies of rehabilitation, I worked every day with patients struggling to regain ground lost to injury and disease. I didn't have to concoct anecdotal scenarios to "spice up" the piece; I was surrounded with them.

# CHAPTER SEVEN

# INCREASING YOUR ODDS OF SUCCESS

Getting an editor's "yes" can be a daunting proposition. But in order to successfully support yourself as a freelance writer, you need to keep the assignments coming. There are a number of ways—tangible and intangible—that you can increase your ratio of "yes's" to "after careful consideration, we regret to inform you's."

## KEEP ABREAST OF THE MARKETS

The market for writing fluctuates constantly. Yesterday's good lead is tomorrow's dead end. The key is simply to pay attention. As we discussed previously, it is important to monitor the trades. Read *Publisher's Weekly*. Read the Markets section of *Writer's Digest*. Spend time browsing the sections of the *Writer's Market* you normally overlook; you'll be surprised at the potential markets you'll discover.

Nearly every writer's publication includes a markets section, but their usefulness varies. It has been my experience that many of the smaller newsletter-type publications frequently list smaller-paying markets or list markets covered with more depth and frequency in larger publications. This is by no means universally true; for instance, *Freelance Success* is a slim, no-frills monthly newsletter, but based on my experience, its current, accurate, and frank listings are well worth the price of subscription.

Different writer's publications cater to different populations of writers, and their market sections often reflect this. The markets highlighted in *Poets & Writers Magazine* are heavily weighted toward fiction and poetry; listings in *ByLine* frequently reflect the readership's interest in spiritual and inspirational themes. While I recommend scanning as many market listings as possible (I review all of the publications I've noted), you can't get them all, so monitor those that most closely parallel your interests and abilities.

Far less orthodox techniques can lead to sales, as well. I rarely make it past a magazine rack without stopping to look for some new niche publication I've missed. The best places for these fishing expeditions are big-city bookstores. Do the same thing in libraries. Beyond discovering titles that may have been missed by the publications you normally rely on, there are additional benefits to trolling magazine racks. First of all, by scanning covers, you get an immediate overview of topics that sell. Even if you've reviewed a magazine's market listings recently, they won't be as recent as what's on this month's cover.

The other advantage to scanning a rack of magazines is visual. Cover photographs say more about a magazine and its audience than any set of writer's guidelines or editorial mission statement. You might think that based on its guidelines you don't have anything to contribute to a trucking magazine, until a celebrity cover catches your eye and you realize you're aware of an untold story involving a celebrity and trucks. It happened to me. Since then I've completed a number of extremely interesting and satisfying assignments for the magazine—all because I did a little "trolling," and because I took the time to become familiar with the publication beyond a quick scan of its entry in *Writer's Market.*

## KEEP AHEAD OF THE REST

Obviously, you won't be the only writer out there scanning the horizon for markets. Many is the time I've seen notes from editors and publishers almost begging for a reprieve from an overwhelming response to their postings. How do you set yourself apart from the crowd of manila envelopes flattening an editor's "In" basket?

**Move Quickly . . .** When you spot a new listing, act on it immediately, before an editor is deluged with a truckload of mail. In other words, the day you read the posting. If you wait more than a day, I can guarantee you will have missed the first wave.

**. . . But Make It a Quality Move.** Because new listings attract a deluge of queries, clips, and resumes, the material you send must stand out from the crowd. Your presentation should be neat and professional. It should be specific to the needs outlined by the editor in the posting. It should demonstrate the range of your abilities (again, with special attention to the specific needs of the target market), but should also be as concise as possible. And always remember; more than your stationery, more than your opinion of yourself, more than *you,* an editor is interested in your *writing.*

## REALLY KNOW YOUR TARGET PUBLICATION

Nothing makes an editor crankier than an inappropriate submission. And based on my reading, there are a lot of cranky editors out there. In interview after interview, they alternately beg and threaten writers to stop sending them ideas that don't match the character of the publication they represent. It's tough enough to successfully pitch a magazine you're familiar with; the idea that so many writers pitch a magazine sight unseen seems ludicrous, but is apparently very common. Simply relying on a market listing is rarely enough. You need to review actual copies of the magazine.

I have seen some editors quoted as saying that a writer who suggests a story done in the past year hasn't been doing his or her homework. We can infer that those editors expect us to be familiar with a minimum of one year's worth of content. Frankly, that's not realistic. It is financially impossible for me to maintain a subscription to every magazine I pitch over the course of a year. Furthermore, if I reviewed an entire year's worth of issues before each pitch, I'd never even fire up the computer. So . . . what's a realistic approach?

**Subscriptions.** As I just pointed out, time and finances limit the viability of this option. However, I do maintain a few subscriptions to magazines I am truly interested in writing for. Reading them each month, I keep in tune with their needs; I also feel challenged to meet the standards they establish. As a side benefit, if they publish good writing, I'll learn something as a writer by reading it.

**Back Issues.** If you wish to pitch a specific publication, a trip to the library to look at back issues isn't a bad idea. In my case, however, "a trip to the library" is a two-hour round trip. Don't forget that back issues of some magazines are available on-line. You can check back issues without leaving home.

**Sample Copies.** This is how I most commonly get familiar with a publication. When I'm in the early stages of composing a proposal, I obtain sample copies of the magazines I have in mind. If a magazine isn't available at a retail outlet near you, check *Writer's Market;* most entries include the price and postage required for sample copies. I keep a file drawer of sample copies for future reference, updating it as needed. If space becomes a problem, consider saving just the cover, table of contents, and a few articles representative of the publication's overall style.

## What to Look For

Once you get your hands on a few copies of a magazine, don't just read it—study it.

- What seems to drive the content of the magazine? What topics are covered? How are they covered? Is the magazine a free-standing entity, or is it an organ of a specific organization?
- Check out the advertisements. What do they say about the magazine's target subscriber?
- How many feature pieces are in each issue? How long are these features? Are there a few mid-range pieces? Does the magazine print small "newsy" items?
- Note the style in which pieces are written. Are they academic? Folksy? Wry? Dry? Whom do the writers seem to be speaking to? Does the magazine itself seem to have a consistent tone or slant? How will that affect your voice, your angle?

When you make your proposal, you'll want to have all of these things in mind. We'll discuss the proposal process in greater detail, but this is a good time to mention that the proposal (usually in the form of a query letter) you send should be composed in a style approximate to the style you would use in writing a piece for the magazine.

## Writer's Guidelines

Writer's guidelines are composed by magazine staff in-house, and go into greater detail than the general market listings you'll find in trade magazines. For instance, writer's guidelines for *The World & I* include information under the following headings: Topics, Content, Format, Style and Tone, Length, Titles, Subheads, Sidebars, Footnoting, Photographs, Illustration, Author's Biography, Items to Accompany the Manuscript, and Payments (our favorite!). In addition to these headings, *The World & I* guidelines include descriptions of the eight major sections of the magazine: Current Issues, The Arts, Natural Science, Life, Book World, Culture, Currents in Modern Thought, and Life and Ideals. The guidelines then go on to break down each section. For instance, the listing of Culture subsections includes paragraphs on Peoples, Crossroads, Folk Wisdom, Heritage, and Patterns/Photo Essay. While the listing for *The World & I* in *Writer's Market* is more extensive than most, it is nowhere near as detailed as the writer's guidelines; this is true for most publications.

Most magazines have a set of writer's guidelines, and will gladly supply you with a copy in return for a stamped, self-addressed envelope. *Hope* magazine makes its extensive writer's guidelines available online, and I suspect others do as well.

Combine what you learn from sample copies of a magazine with what you are told in the writer's guidelines, and you'll greatly increase your chances of coming up with a proposal that will get an editor's attention.

## Editorial Calendars

Some magazines plan their issues up to a year in advance. Even in the case of the smallest magazines, it's unsafe to assume that the editor isn't working four to six months in advance. When you request writer's guidelines, request an editorial calendar. If the magazine sends one, study it and stow it away in your brain; in addition to actively seeking out material to match the calendar, you never know when you'll happen upon something appropriate.

Better three months early than three days late.

## PRESENT YOURSELF AS A PROFESSIONAL

Nothing will help you find success like an intimate familiarity with your target market. But while your focus is directed toward the publication, its editor, and its audience, don't forget to focus on yourself.

Essentially, when you are approaching an editor in the hope of writing a piece for that editor's magazine, you're engaging in a job interview. Present yourself appropriately. In most cases that has nothing to do with shiny shoes and a tie (I own neither), but with preparedness and thoroughness. An editor should sense that you've done your homework. That you can deliver the goods. That you're serious about delivering good work. From avoiding typos in your correspondence to crafting a lean, focused proposal, everything you can do to make an editor see that you view writing as a professional vocation rather than a quirky avocation will increase your odds of success.

## FIND THE ANGLE

More than the topic, editors are interested in the "angle." Think about the number of times you've seen references to your (potential) sex life on the cover of *Cosmopolitan.* The writers who propose those articles don't just propose another article on sex, they come up with a specific—pardon me—*angle.* The editors of *Seattle Weekly* aren't interested in an article on pottery. They may, however, be interested in an article on pottery shops in the Seattle area, or a profile of a Seattle potter. You get the idea.

Learn to look for the things everyone else is missing. While covering a large outdoor country music event, I noticed how everyone strained to catch a glimpse of the stars riding in the opulent buses pulling in and out of the grounds. It struck me that the best story wasn't about the overexposed celebrity, but about the person behind the wheel of the bus. Eventually I was able to write a piece about one of these characters.

Perhaps, in addition to learning to look for the thing everyone else is missing, it is equally important to look at the thing everyone else is seeing and put a twist on it.

### MISSING, PRESUMED SALABLE

Speaking at a recent writer's conference, *National Geographic* editor Priit Vesilind recommended that writers who "look for holes in our coverage" stand the best chance of landing an assignment. In other words, while scanning magazines to see what's there, keep in mind that it may be equally important to note what's *not* there.

## HELP YOUR EDITOR GET THE PICTURE

Many editors are more inclined to view your proposals favorably if you can provide illustrations or photos. Early in my freelance writing career, I collaborated with an artist friend who provided an illustration for one of my articles. We then went on to supply illustrations to several other articles. I have also illustrated several of my own humor pieces for a regional magazine.

I have also supplied photographs for several of my own articles, and in a few cases, I know that my ability to supply those photos influenced the editor to accept my piece nearly as much as my writing or the subject matter.

A word of caution: When an editor asks if I can provide photographs, I am very careful not to get in over my head. I make it very clear to the editor that I am not a professional photographer—to say otherwise would be misleading, ultimately ill-advised, and insulting to the number of fine professional photographers who have provided wonderful images for my articles in the past.

### MUST I HAVE A COMPUTER?

No, you don't have to own a computer. And you don't have to own a car. Or a telephone. But if you want to freelance, you are at an extreme disadvantage without these things. I started with a legal pad and a manual typewriter. I still use the legal pads. But . . .

- A computer and a decent printer generate neat, clean copy. And when necessary, they generate multiple copies (of query letters or articles) quickly and painlessly.
- Most articles must be a certain length; a word count function in your word processing program can keep you up-to-date with length as often as you wish.
- With little more than the click of a mouse, I can access an encyclopedia, dictionary, almanac, a book of quotations, a chronology, and atlas, and—though I hate to admit ever going there—a thesaurus.
- Among other resources, *Writer's Market* is now available on CD-ROM. While I have found the first edition a bit slow and clunky, I love the ability to perform cross-referenced searches in a relatively short amount of time. Previously, these searches required an afternoon of poring over the print version, flipping back and forth between the index and the main text.
- Tracking submissions with a computer is a breeze; I have my own simple setup (described in Chapter Thirteen), but tracking programs are available also.
- More and more of my freelance assignments involve electronic communication, from e-mail communications with editors to several magazines that download my manuscripts directly from an electronic file.
- Finally, although I am grumpily inclined to dismiss ninety-nine percent of the hyper-hyped Internet as a glorified chat line, I must admit that it has become a powerful research tool, further enabling me to hide out in my tiny town and yet maintain contact with the outside world.

If computers scare you, think of them the way I do: as a high-tech typewriter/filing cabinet. My computer knowledge is decidedly minimal, and yet I find my way around with only the occasional frustrating impasse. With each day that passes, these silicon machines are dumbed down closer and closer to the level at which we non-techies operate. I must say that it took some getting used to at first, but upon reflection, the transition from typewriter to computer was no more traumatic than the transition from legal pads to manual typewriter. I still do some longhand writing when I'm on the road, but I now prefer to write on computer. I like the percussive rhythm of writing on a keyboard, and when it comes to rewriting, I'd sure hate to give up the computer-given ability to manipulate text, move chunks here and there, and keep old drafts for comparison.

I am aware of a few fairly well-known and undeniably successful writers who still bash away at a manual typewriter or write longhand. Uncowed by the relentless advance of technology, they face it down with firm resolve—and in most cases, with an assistant . . . who owns a computer.

## REJECTION IS PART OF THE GAME

Rejection. It's part of every writer's life. Why am I discussing rejection in a chapter about success? Because how you handle rejection will have a direct effect on that success.

Now then. It's quite possible my tone in the paragraphs that follow may offend a few folks. I don't mean to. I'm a relatively pleasant fellow when actually flushed out into the sunlight. But I have to tell you, I've read more than my share of essays on rejection, how it hurts, how one must overcome it to press on, how it stalks the edges of writers' dreams, and so on. I've lost track of the number of times I've been informed by someone at a party (twice, I suppose, based on my party attendance rate over the past few years) that they want to send their writing out, but, "I just don't know if I can handle the rejection."

Quite frankly, I don't understand what all the fuss is about. Based on the sheer numbers of folks who would be writers, combined with the relatively minute market for writing, combined with the highly esoteric needs of that market, combined with the infinite number of reasons an editor has for not needing a particular piece of writing, the likelihood that one's work might be rejected seems likely indeed, integral to the process, and not at all emotionally damaging. All part of the job, in other words.

Rejection has nothing to do with you the person. It may have something to do with you the writer, but unless you've gone out of your way to stand out from the crowd in a mighty contrary way, an editor will very rarely return your manuscript because he or she finds you personally repulsive. No, the reasons for rejection lie elsewhere, and are myriad. Here, off the top of my head, are just a few:

- The topic you propose has recently been addressed by the publication.
- The topic is not appropriate for this particular market.
- The manuscript was sloppily presented.
- Your proposal was chock full of typos.
- The article you wrote and submitted was too long.
- The article you wrote and submitted was too short.
- The editorial calendar is full.
- Your proposal fails to address the magazine's target audience.
- The editor to whom you sent your material quit.
- The editor was cross promoted.
- The editor died (it happens—been there).

Note that missing from the list is "The editor hates you." If you are fortunate enough to attain a level of notoriety at which editors are rejecting your work because of their personal dislike for you, it's time to get an agent.

OK. So your proposed article on courting rituals of the newt has been rejected. What now? Noodling morosely about the house, contemplating your navel or the bottom of your teacup, is a luxury, which, should you some day "make it," will provide great copy for your biography. In the meantime, if you're serious about this writing business, you will recognize that rejection of a piece one place is merely permission to sell it elsewhere. Rejection means you're in the game. It means you're getting the work done and you're getting it out there. I am always surprised when I meet people I know to be talented writers and they express wonder at my ability to make a living at this business. And yet, when I speak further with them, I learn that their stuff isn't out there circulating. When your "stuff" comes back in the mail with regrets, send it back out that day.

You will also learn to judge the quality of your rejections. Yes, some rejections are better than others. Most come in the form of a slip of paper that reads as follows:

> We regret that we are unable to use the enclosed material. Thank you for giving us the opportunity to consider it.
>
> —*the editors*

(Actually, that rejection is quoted verbatim from a *The New Yorker* rejection slip. Never mind how I came to possess it.)

So—that's your average heartless rejection. But sometimes you get a slip with a little note elaborating on why the piece was rejected. Sometimes an editor will encourage you to refocus the piece and submit it again. The point is, as busy as editors are, they don't spend a lot of time jotting personal notes to writers they don't know. If you earn a comment—even in rejection—it tells you that your work earned more than cursory editorial attention. That's a good sign. It means you're headed in the right direction.

Occasionally, an editor will send a rejection but recommend other publications that may be interested in the piece. If so, act on these recommendations in good haste.

# CHAPTER EIGHT

# THE QUERY LETTER

One of the greatest means of getting an editor's attention is the query letter. Short of buying the publishing company, nothing increases your chances of getting an article published like a good query letter.

Essentially, the query letter is a proposal. It is your chance to meet privately with an editor and say, "Here is my idea for an article . . . if you like the idea, I will write it for you."

The alternative to submitting a query letter is to write and submit a finished article.

## WHY YOU SHOULD QUERY

There are several reasons why you're better off to query first:

1. **Query letters are the industry standard.** A quick scan of *The Writer's Market* will reveal that nearly all editors prefer to see a query letter, and some refuse to even look at "unsolicited" articles.
2. **Query letters get you noticed.** Even if a magazine accepts unsolicited articles, they are placed in a "slush pile." A slush pile is a towering stack of unread manuscripts teetering precariously in some corner of an editor's office. Many editors make an honest effort to plow through these slush piles, but the odds of your piece being selected are infinitesimal. The odds of your concise query letter being read and responded to are very good.

3. **Query letters are time-savers.** In the time it takes to research and write just one article on one topic, you can generate several queries on several topics.
4. **Query letters help you maximize precious writing time.** By querying an editor before writing an article, you can save yourself the trouble of writing and polishing an article for which there is no market—or the trouble of writing an article on a topic that just ran in last month's issue!
5. **Query letters get you "inside" information.** Should you beat the odds and an editor finds your unsolicited article attractive, she may want a different slant. She may want a different style. It may be too long or short. By querying first, you would have been able to tailor the piece to the market from the beginning.
6. **Query letters allow you to blanket the market.** Because they are easily modified, query letters allow you to approach a number of markets in a short time.
7. **Query letters serve as your resume.** A query letter is your opportunity to prove to an editor that you have the skill and knowledge he is looking for.

## WHEN NOT TO QUERY

There are times when a query is inappropriate or unnecessary, and occasionally an editor does prefer to see a complete manuscript. For instance, unless you are a nationally recognized humorist, no editor is going to buy a humorous piece from you based on a query letter, no matter how well-written. You'll still have to prove your wit by writing the piece. The same is true for essays, columns of personal opinion, and most fiction.

A good rule of thumb: If the success of the piece you have in mind depends on nuances of tone and style—rather than facts, quotes, and general reportage—then it may be best to skip the query letter.

Before you send out a completed manuscript to more than one publisher, please see the "Simultaneous Submissions" section in this chapter.

## IS A COVER LETTER MORE APPROPRIATE?

In some cases in which a query letter is inappropriate or unnecessary, a cover letter may be your answer. Some publications request a cover letter with all manuscript submissions, solicited or unsolicited. Check their writer's guidelines to be sure. A cover letter is generally a concise note introducing the piece and providing pertinent biographical information about you.

If I am submitting an essay, a humor piece, or an unsolicited manuscript, I include a cover letter simply because it provides an editor with a quick synopsis (usually no longer than a paragraph) of the submitted material along the lines of style and topic. Since editors don't have time to read everything they receive, I want the chance to say, "Enclosed for your consideration is a humorous essay on how one contemporary male is dealing with impending baldness" in the opening paragraph of my cover letter rather than assuming an editor will work his or her way through my lead and into the essay to determine this on his or her own. It's still up to me to be funny, but if my research is correct, I'll have gotten the editor's attention by mentioning a topic the magazine is interested in, and will be given a fair read.

I've included some examples of cover letters in this chapter. The comments accompanying each will further explain when and why they are useful.

## QUERYING BY E-MAIL

Some publications are now accepting even unsolicited queries by e-mail, although regular or "snail mail" continues to be preferred. A number of the magazines I work with will accept my queries via e-mail. In some cases, I follow the guidelines of ordinary query letter composition; in other cases, I simply dash off a paragraph and send it out on the wires—but that informality is dictated by the relationship more than the medium.

## DON'T QUERY BY FAX OR PHONE

Unless you have an express invitation to do so, don't query by fax. If you do, the same rules of composition apply as when you are mailing a query.

Querying by phone is also virtually always a no-no. Unless you've established a strong relationship with an editor, or phone queries are accepted as a matter of policy, you stand a fine chance of simply irritating the person you least want to irritate.

Even with the handful of editors who accept my phone calls, I still prefer to pitch my projects in writing. As much as I love words, I am not the most articulate person in the world when it comes to speaking on the phone. I don't *umm* and *aah,* but I often leave gaps of silence between words while I think about where I'm headed. I tend to over-explain and go off on tangents. None of this is beneficial when speaking to a harried editor.

## COMPOSING A QUERY LETTER

A query letter should be as carefully crafted as your finest finished article. After all, a query letter introduces you to the editor and is the basis upon which he or she will form a critical first impression of you as a writer. If you are a beginner without publication credits, the query letter is your chance to showcase your writing ability.

Ninety-nine percent of the time, a query letter should be limited to one page. Anything longer is likely to receive less than an editor's full attention—remember, most editors sort through thousands of these things. Your goal is to interest the editor in the topic; not bury him with information. In addition, a long query letter may suggest to an editor that you lack the ability to edit yourself—a critical skill for all writers. The finest advice I have ever heard on this subject comes from Colleen Mohyde, a literary agent speaking at a nonfiction writer's conference: "It's not how long the query letter *is,* it's how long it *seems.*"

While it is appropriate to allow your personality to come through, the tone of the letter should be professional and respectful; conversational but not casual.

### READ SOME BOOK FLAPS

Literary agent Colleen Mohyde tells would-be authors composing a book proposal they should think in terms of book jacket copy; this excellent advice is also worth applying to your magazine queries.

## To Whom Do I Address My Query?

Generally, your query should be directed to the articles editor. However, some magazines have different editors for different sections. The names of these editors can be obtained from sources including the *Writer's Market* or *Literary Market Place,* or from the masthead of the publication itself.

If you want to be absolutely sure your query is directed to the proper person, phone the magazine. Popular listings and mastheads may not reflect the changes in personnel that happen all too often in the publishing world. Don't simply fire your proposal off to the editor at the top of the masthead. Editors come and go, and a quick phone call to a magazine's editorial offices will not only save you trouble, it can pay off handsomely. You can usually get all the information you need from the receptionist; describe (briefly!) your topic, and ask to whom the proposal should be addressed.

A hint: If you are still unsure who should get your submission, you might do well to address the material to the attention of the assistant editor rather than the editor. The assistant editor may not have as much power to assign a project, but chances are, he or she gets less mail and will take more time to read your query or article.

## How Do I Open?

Everyone agrees that the opening line of a query letter is critically important. There is disagreement, however, among "experts" as to what form the opening line should take. Many feel you should begin with a bang, opening with a "grabber." On the other hand, some editors grow weary of writers trying to "grab" them and would prefer a simple, straightforward statement relating the importance and appeal of the topic for the magazine's readers.

Ultimately, you must follow your instincts. A great opening line will grab an editor's attention and showcase your ability to write outstanding copy; on the other hand, a poorly crafted, cutesy opener may lose the editor before you've even broached your subject.

One thing is certain: whether you go for a grabber or choose a simple statement, skip the small talk and get right to the point. This is not the place for a long, involved setup.

## Then What?

The form your query letter takes at this point will depend on your topic and your individual style. Depending on your purposes, you should include or accomplish the following:

**The Proposal.** The query letter should clearly describe the type of article you intend to write, including the topic and scope of the piece. What will it be about? What will the article accomplish for the reader? Establish (through implication, not outright declaration!—see the "Do's and Don'ts . . ." sidebar) that the article will be of interest or value to the magazine's readership.

**The Angle.** It's not enough to approach an editor with a broad topic; your query letter must demonstrate that you intend to examine a unique aspect of the topic. You must know the *story*. Rather than simply saying, "I'm going to be in Belize . . . would you like a story about Belize?" you need to tell an editor what you're going to do with your experience; how you're going to turn it into a story relevant to the publication being queried. When I knew I would be in Belize, I queried a fire-fighting journal and asked if they would be interested in a piece on the status of Belizean fire-fighting techniques and equipment. In reading about the country, I learned that a number of Confederate soldiers had settled there after the Civil War; as a result, I queried a Civil War magazine and asked if they would be interested in a piece on the settlement and what had become of it.

**Timeliness.** Is there a reason this article should be written now? Is it tied to current events? Is it a seasonal piece (see sidebar, "Seasonal Queries").

**Style.** A query letter should always be professional. In some cases, however, it is appropriate to alter your style to reflect the market you are approaching. If the magazine in question has a wry, postmodern, satirical style, it might not hurt to compose your query letter in a wry, postmodern, satirical style. Use your intuition, but always remember: The minute your style interferes with your message, you lose.

**Shopping List.** A bulleted list of article highlights is a good way to present the meat of your proposal in a clear, concise manner.

**Knowledge of Topic.** Your query should reflect a good understanding of the topic you propose to write about. Demonstrate that you have an insight about the subject that is unique or greater than that of the average person. Tell the editor why you are the person to write this piece. Write with a tone of capable authority; you must *sound* as if you're the person for the job as much as you *say* you're the person for the job. (Don't interpret this advice as a license to brag; see the "Do's and Don'ts . . ." sidebar).

**Sources.** Give an editor assurance that you have access to current information; describe how and where (and from whom) you plan to obtain the information.

**Quotations.** Quotations about the proposed topic by experts in the field, potential interview subjects, or public figures can catch an editor's eye if they are used judiciously. Just make sure they're appropriate, concise, and not overabundant.

**Sidebars.** Sidebars are usually developed late in the writing/research stage. However, if you have a strong sidebar idea you may wish to mention it in your query.

**Artwork/Photographs.** Depending on the nature of the article, indicate your ability to supply artwork or photographs.

**Autobiographical Information.** A little information about who you are right at the beginning or at the very end of a query is important, but don't get carried away. Stick to noting a few of your publishing credits and anything that qualifies you to write the piece—a paragraph at most, or salt them in the main text: "While working on a piece for *Newsweek,* I learned that. . . ."

**Clips.** If your work has been published previously, include a few samples. This gives an editor an idea of your abilities. Select your clips appropriately; don't just sling everything you've got in an envelope. If possible they should reflect the style of writing the editor is interested in. If an editor has sent out the call for writers who can compose a treatise on the socioeconomic impact of Reconstruction on the Post-War South, that editor probably isn't interested in a clip of your humorous essay on the woes of camping in the rain with three preschoolers and a bear.

If you haven't been previously published, you may wish to include samples of unpublished writing. Just remember: the query letter itself is the most critical piece of writing you will include in the envelope.

**SASE (Self-Addressed, Stamped Envelope).** Always, *always* include a SASE for an editor's reply. If you submit photographs or clips with your query, be sure the postage on your SASE is adequate for their return.

## Do's and Don'ts for Query Letters

**Don't**

- Don't try to sell yourself by saying, "This is the article you've been waiting for!"; "Your readers are going to love this!" Phrases like these sound amateurish, *are* amateurish, and will get you absolutely nowhere with seasoned editors. As a matter of fact, such hucksterism amounts to your committing a grave insult by telling an editor you know better than he or she what the readership wants. The editor will look for proof in your pudding, not your PR.
- Don't use strange, hard-to-read type fonts: When editors want strange, hard-to-read fonts, they hire graphic designers.
- Don't use right or center justification: It's difficult to read.
- Don't use all capital letters: Making an editor read "all caps" is like shouting at someone suffering a hangover.
- Don't promise anything you can't deliver: ". . . then I plan to interview the President and his three extraterrestrial cousins."

**Do**

- Proofread scrupulously.
- Write as carefully as if the query were the article itself.
- Be familiar with your target publication.
- Demonstrate that you are familiar with the topic.
- Show that you have access to "inside" information.
- Pitch an angle, not a topic

## IS THERE ANYTHING I SHOULDN'T INCLUDE IN A QUERY?

There is usually no need to include a title for your proposed article. When it comes to factors that will influence an editor to approve your article, he is far less interested in your ability to come up with a cute title than a complete article. (For more on choosing titles for your articles, see Chapter Eleven.)

If your article is approved, the editor will let you know how long it should be and assign you a deadline, so there is no need to include your suggestions in a query.

And finally, this is not the time to inform an editor how much money you are willing to accept for your writing. These things are worked out after an editor decides to offer you the assignment. If you are in a position to dictate your rates in a query letter, you don't need this book, you need to get writing!

### SEASONAL QUERIES

Think ahead when you query. Way ahead. Don't send out your pitch for a proposed piece on the history of tinsel in November. Remember, even small magazines are usually working four to six months in advance. I've written for magazines that set their editorial calendar a year in advance. Find out if the magazine has an editorial calendar and request a copy. You might also check *Writer's Market,* as most magazines indicate how much lead time they require for pieces with a seasonal tie-in.

## THE EXCEPTIONS TO THE RULES

Of course, there are exceptions to every rule. Just as with the rest of your writing, you will develop your own style for writing query letters. In some cases, the style of the query letter is dictated by the style of publication you are querying. As you become familiar with certain editors, you may tailor queries to match their personalities. By and large, however, the standard elements of a good query letter remain the same: specificity, clarity, and brevity.

One further comment about breaking the rules. Among the examples of actual query letters included in this chapter are a few that run over the one-page limit. I can assure you, however, that this is a very rare exception, and not recommended unless you have a very solid reason for doing so.

### Editor Alan Burdick on Query Letters

*The New York Times Magazine* editor Alan Burdick makes the following recommendations for query letters:

> "First of all, address your query to the appropriate editor *by name.* Then, keep in mind these four points:

1. Know your audience. Read the publication before you query.
2. Send clips.
3. I want to hear your 'voice' in the query letter.
4. Substance. Do you have a *story*? Do you have *news*? I need to know that your story contains the elements of character, voice, mood, tension, narrative."

## MULTIPLE QUERIES

Should you send out the same query to more than one magazine? You bet. If you've got a strong idea for an article you think might be appropriate for more than one magazine—especially if the piece is time-sensitive—there's no sense in sending out one query at a time and then waiting for a rejection to trickle in weeks or months later before sending out the next. Some editors disagree, but as far as I'm concerned it's a freelancing necessity. When I do make a multiple query, however, I print the words *multiple simultaneous query* or *limited simultaneous query* very clearly in the lower right-hand corner of my query letter. That way, everything's out in the open and aboveboard.

## SIMULTANEOUS SUBMISSIONS

If you offer the same piece of writing to more than one publication at the same time, you are making a simultaneous submission. This is dicey territory if you don't take the right steps. The potential problem actually arrives in the form of good fortune: Two editors call, both offering to purchase the piece. You are in the position of telling the second editor that you've already sold the piece, perhaps after that editor went to the mat or reserved space for the piece.

Most magazines state clearly in their writer's guidelines whether or not they accept simultaneous submissions. *Writer's Market* listings also note when a magazine is willing to accept simultaneous submissions.

I make simultaneous submissions as a matter of course. Like multiple queries, it's a freelancing necessity. Sometimes a piece is too timely, or the rent is too soon due, to be sent to one market at a time and rejected at leisure. Even if it isn't time-sensitive, heck, I just want my stuff out there in front of as many eyes as possible.

If a magazine says it doesn't accept simultaneous submissions, I generally respect their wishes. But not always. I simply do not believe the risk is that great. If the piece you send is just what that editor is looking for, it won't be rejected just because you let someone else peek at it too. Yes, if two editors come after the same piece, there might be a bit of grumbling, but I would look upon that kind of luck and interest as a positive omen.

But here's the key: Never send out a simultaneous submission—whether it be to a publication that officially accepts them or not—without clearly stating on your cover letter or the manuscript that the piece the editor is holding has been sent to other desks as well.

## Cage-Rattling Etiquette

There is no hard-and-fast rule on how long you should wait to hear from an editor regarding your query before sending a follow-up note. As a general rule, I wait three or four weeks before sending a polite note. In some cases, if the editor is someone I've worked with, I'll make a follow-up call a week to two weeks after sending the query, but this is usually prearranged. I'd have to say that in most cases, a phone call follow-up should be a last resort. Editors don't care to be bothered at work by strangers any more than you do.

And then, as always, there are the exceptions. *National Geographic* editor Priit Vesilind says he prefers writers contact him *before* sending their query. His magazine's specific needs and distinct style make it a very tough sell, and he can save himself and the writer time with a quick yes or no before the query is crafted.

### STATIONERY

Your stationery should be understated and professional. Please, no writerly dingbats or uplifting quotations or curlicues or nature scenes or embossed coffee mug stains. Or, as one editor put it, "nothing that says 'writer.' " This is not to say that you can't make an impression; but make it subtly. I think it's a good idea that your stationery be clearly identifiable (my envelopes and letterhead bear a small logo of a polka-dotted Holstein in a cow-crossing sign), but not overpowering (my envelopes and letter stock are plain old white, my address and contact information are in an unadorned font). Remember, it's your *material* that should make you stand out from the crowd. Goldleaf stationery with a fully illuminated return address sent in an envelope that, when opened, emits confetti and the sound of applause will attract attention, but will only heighten an editor's disappointment if the contents of your submission are overshadowed by your dancing envelope.

## SAMPLE QUERY LETTERS

Each of the following letters resulted in a sale. Beyond that, they share very little similarity in execution, style, or technique. Even though they were successful, they are imperfect; in a few cases, I'll point out something I'd change if I had it to do over again. In one case, I marvel that I made the sale at all. Reading your old query letters can be every bit as embarrassing as reading your old poems. I sometimes find myself wondering just who was responsible for the mawkish yawping on the page before me, and I never hesitate when given the opportunity to take a shot at myself.

I'm so easy to hit.

**LETTER 1 Straightforward Nonfiction Query**

Kathryn Fanning
*ByLine*
P.O. Box 130596
Edmond, OK 73013

Dear Ms. Fanning:

(1) As a freelance writer and recent subscriber to *ByLine*, I have been impressed by the straightforward, helpful information that is contained in each issue. You manage to consistently produce "fluff-free" articles that are truly an asset to those of us eking out a living from the keyboard.

(2) Having offered my thanks, I would also like to offer an article proposal. In my work as a freelancer (I have enclosed a resume), I have discovered a rich resource that is often overlooked: corporate libraries.

(3) A surprising number of these libraries exist in any given town, and most can be accessed by the public. Corporate libraries offer a number of unique advantages (4) to the freelancer:

(5)
- Extensive, in-depth information on "niche" topics.
- Texts and journals often unavailable in public libraries.

*(Continued)*

- Many have computerized search capabilities available for a nominal fee, as well as interlibrary loan services.

- Many of the topic-specific and obscure journals found in corporate libraries are not included in popular market listings. In addition, technical or research articles often address a topic that can be retailored for a more general market, and the scholars who penned the pieces are excellent interview contacts.

⑤

⑥ As someone who has used corporate libraries extensively, I can attest to the fact that they are a largely untapped resource for writers. Would *ByLine* be interested in a piece on the topic?

⑦ I thank you for your time and consideration and look forward to your reply.

Sincerely,
Michael Perry

⑧ P.S. I have enclosed a copy of an article about corporate libraries that I wrote for a local business journal.

## Comments, Letter 1

1. The opening sentence demonstrates that I am familiar with the publication. It also mentions that I am a freelance writer; the second sentence (if a bit melodramatically) establishes that I freelance for a living. This establishes my qualifications for writing the piece I have yet to propose.

There is a fine line between demonstrating your familiarity with a publication (which is important) and outright ingratiation. I think I'd tone it down a bit today, but I remember how hungry I was for guidance when I wrote this letter, and early on in my career I found plenty in *ByLine,* so every word was true, if a bit earnest.

2. Now a transition. "Here is why I am sending this letter." Rather than go for a "grabber," or convolute my way to the point, I have simply stated my intent. In the second sentence I establish (again, this time with a resume, no less ) that I have something in common with the magazine's readership, and that I have discovered something that readership might wish to know more about.

3. This sentence makes it clear (if a tad optimistically) that the topic is widely relevant.

4. "Unique advantages" suggests to the editor why her readers might care about the topic.

5. Bullets. Presenting the meat of the proposal in a clear, concise manner. Also suggesting that the article might contain bulleted items; something I knew this particular magazine frequently included in its pieces.

6. One more plug for my specific qualifications to write the piece.

7. Superfluous? Could be. It's just that . . . well . . . I *mean* that. To this day, I conclude most of my queries with this phrase.

8. While this clip didn't reflect the style *ByLine* was interested in, it did give the editor an opportunity to further judge the usefulness of the topic, as well as my ability to deliver.

Why did I put the information in postscript? It seemed distracting in the body of the piece.

**LETTER 2 Query for a Profile**

Paul L. Hayden
*Lake Superior Magazine*
Lake Superior Port Cities, Inc.
P.O. Box 16417
Duluth, MN 55816-0417

Dear Mr. Hayden:

(1) Joe Lindzius is a mighty colorful character. His business card features a cartoon of a man in full song behind a drum set, drumming with one hand and tossing a pizza crust with the other. The card reads, "Joe Lindzius—Drums, Vocals & Pizza."

(2) "Solid Joe," as he is known to his friends and fans, cut his musical teeth in the blues and jazz clubs of Chicago, backing up many of the big names. Feeling a need for the peace and quiet of the northwoods, he packed up his drum sticks and headed north, settling in (3) Iron River, Wisconsin. There he opened a pizza parlor, which remains a popular spot to this day.

(4) Joe's retreat has been disrupted, however, by the success of Molly and the Heymakers, a country band based in Hayward. Joe is the drummer for the Heymakers, who have had two (5) Top 40 hits and a Top 10 video in the past year and are scheduled to release their next single and first album early next year.

*(Continued)*

⑥ On stage Joe is known for his "solid" drumming skills, his clowning, and his ability to dance and sing while banging out a rhythm. Off stage he makes delicious pizza and prowls the waters around Iron River in search of monster crappies.

⑦ Would you be interested in an article on Solid Joe?

⑧ I have enclosed an article I did earlier this year on the Heymakers for *Wisconsin West.* The piece should give you an idea of my style and also contains more information on Joe and the band.

⑨ I have written for numerous national and regional markets, including *The Christian Science Monitor,* and have authored two humor books. Please do not hesitate to contact me at either number above if you require further information.

Sincerely,
Michael Perry

## Comments, Letter 2

1. Joe did all the work for me here. The minute he handed me his card, I had everything I needed for a nice introductory paragraph. As a matter of fact, I should have skipped the "mighty colorful character" line and cut straight to the card. Nonetheless, the result was a mild form of the "grabber" lead.

2. Now I summarize Joe's life (as it is relevant to the piece) in three sentences.

3. *Lake Superior Magazine* will only consider topics from a very specific geographical area. The early reference to Iron River lets the editor know the geographical qualification has been met.

4. This is the story.

5. Provides a national angle on a local subject.

6. This is the character.

7. People in sales call it "Going for the close."

8. Clips are good. Relevant clips are even better.

9. Quick credits. Brevity is best.

**LETTER 3 Extended, Stylistic Query**

Daryln Brewer, Editor
*Poets & Writers Magazine*
72 Spring Street
New York, NY 10012

Dear Editor Brewer:

(1) Something's going on in Eau Claire, Wisconsin—and has been for some time.

(2) Eau Claire is a town built on sawdust. In the late 1800s, lumberjacks to the north felled white pines by the millions. Bucked into manageable lengths, the trees were sent south on the Eau Claire and Chippewa rivers, herded along by "river rats" who danced across their lengths in caulked boots, coaxing reluctant logs downstream with thrusts of their slender pike poles. Downstream, where the Eau Claire and "Mighty Chip" converged, a sawmill waited. Here the logs were pooled until they could be sawed into the planks used to build a young nation. It was at this convergence that the City of Eau Claire was born.

Today, the lumber barons who grew rich on the backs of the 'jacks, the river rats, and the sawyers are gone. Most of their mansions have been subdivided into apartments, many of which are rented by students who come to this

*(Continued)*

(2) relatively small town to attend the University of Wisconsin–Eau Claire. Over the years, the whine of the sawmills has been supplanted by other sounds: sounds of large and small industry; sounds of manufacture and construction; sounds of the descendants of river rats and sawyers building a community largely blue-collar and conservative in character.

(3) Perhaps then it will surprise some to learn that one of the most consistent sounds to be heard in Eau Claire for many years has been the sound of poetry; of literature. This brings us to what has been "going on" in Eau Claire. Consider:

(4)

(6) • In recent years, the number of Wisconsin Arts Board grants awarded to writers from Eau Claire has been significantly greater than those awarded to writers from the city of Milwaukee or the city (and cultural center) of Madison.

(5) • A brief list of a few of the award-winning writers with Eau Claire ties includes poet Bruce Taylor (1993 winner of a Bush Artists Foundation Fellowship); Dick Terrill (Associated Writing Program award for nonfiction); Debra Frigan-Munroe (Flannery O'Connor Award for Short Stories); and Ruth Olson (Stanford University's Wallace Stegner Award).

*(Continued)*

④ ⑤

• *N.O.T.A.* (None Of The Above), the UW–Eau Claire literary magazine, has been recognized nationally, placing first and second in the Coordinating Council of Literary Magazines competition.

• The N.O.T.A. open poetry reading held on the UW–Eau Claire campus is one of the most well-attended, longest-running series in the United States. "The crowds it draws (100 to 120 persons per monthly reading) rival those in Chicago and New York," says Bruce Taylor, who originated the series and remembers the first open reading: "There were four people in the audience; three readers and my wife!" Since then, audiences have grown dramatically, and attendance is consistently high. "We had one reading that featured the poetry of four generations from one family," says Taylor. Professor Christian Knoeller, who obtained his Ph.D. from Berkeley and only recently arrived in Eau Claire, was pleasantly surprised by the popularity of the readings, noting that attendance exceeded readings he participated in at both Berkeley and Yale.

I submit these items not in a spirit of boastfulness. Rather, I submit them for your consideration, suggesting that there is a story to be told here; a story of literature being created and appreciated in what some would characterize as an unlikely spot.

*(Continued)*

⑦ Would you be interested in such a piece for *Poets & Writers Magazine*? There are a number of interesting angles to be pursued, including what it is about this small northern town that nurtures an appreciation and development of the writing craft (told through the eyes of some of the writers themselves, perhaps); the relationship of the flow of writers who have passed through this town to the river that flows, literally, through the city and university campus; and a visit to, and history of, the perennially successful N.O.T.A. readings.

I would welcome the opportunity to discuss this proposal further. I can be contacted at either of the numbers above, or via the enclosed SASE.

A brief summary of my writing credits is also enclosed.

Thank you for your time and consideration. I look forward to your reply.

Sincerely,
Mike Perry

## Comments, Letter 3

Now we're getting to an example of a letter that breaks some rules. The most obvious rule being flaunted is the mandate that queries not extend beyond a single page. I knew, however, that in order to interest a national magazine in this fairly local story, I'd need to make a strong case for its relevance. I believe my willingness to chance breaking the "one page" rule allowed me to do that.

Second, *Poets & Writers Magazine* is one of those wonderful publications that allows you—and encourages—a certain amount of "voice" in your work. In a sense, I viewed the query as an audition. I wanted to make the case for the content, but I also wanted to demonstrate my stylistic intentions.

Chancy? Yes.

Do it every time? Of course not.

Did it work? Yes.

1. *What's* going on? I'm banking on the editor's interest. A variation on the "grabber" technique.

2. Auditioning my prose. When I wrote the query, I envisioned this as the lead for the published story. As it turned out, I cut all this history and river setup, led off the piece with an epigraph from *Rolling Stone,* and set the opening scene in a bar. So much for art.

3. The story.

4. Once again, bullets. Unlike the case of the *ByLine* query, a *Poets & Writers Magazine* regional profile is not likely to contain bulleted items; however, it seemed the most clear and expeditious way to go about making my case. They support the story.

5. Each of these bullets serves to widen the relevance of what is primarily a regional topic, giving it national relevance.

6. Each bulleted item reflects my willingness to do some research. In the context of the query letter, that research primarily serves to support my proposal; it serves a larger purpose by showing that I am committed to writing something more than a simple puff piece about a local writer's group. However, an admission: Further research (after I received the assignment) showed that the source of my information for this first item was slightly inaccurate. All the more reason to hang your story on more than one peg.

7. After "going for the close," I offer angles and possibilities. This demonstrates that I have given good thought to the piece, but remain flexible.

**LETTER 4 Informal Piggy-Backed Paragraph**

Item number two: ① One of my annual freelance "gigs" involves my covering Country Fest, ② a four-day bash in a cow pasture that involves over 30 country music acts, a plethora of egregious fashion errors (cowboy boots with shorts, lime green tube tops, that sort of thing), oceans of beer, and anywhere from 20,000 to 30,000 festgoers per day, many with their own RV, tent, or trailer. As you might expect, fire and EMS personnel are on scene 'round the clock. ③ Would you be interested in a piece about what it takes to protect this temporary city in the country? ④ The photo possibilities are above average, to say the least. ⑤ Last year the festival was smashed by a severe windstorm that collapsed tents and part of the staging. ⑥ A recap of the response would make a great sidebar.

## Comments, Letter 4

If you've cultivated a good relationship with an editor, your queries may take on an informal air. Don't be lulled: You still need to pack a punch.

Letter 4 is a one-paragraph query taken from a letter to the editor of *911 Magazine.* I piggy-packed the paragraph in a letter taking care of some business with a previous assignment.

1. I'll be there anyway . . .

2. Set the scene. In this case, I'm pitching to a magazine that concerns itself with fire and emergency medical services (EMS). I know that if I can find a fire and EMS *story* outside the usual fire and EMS *setting,* I'll increase my odds of getting the assignment. In other words, a story about firefighters battling fires might be of interest; a story about firefighters surrounded by inebriated country music fans is likely of greater interest.

3. The story in a nutshell.

4. Does the magazine like photos? Increase your odds of making the sale by supplying pictures to accompany your story. If those pictures involve lime green tube tops, the editor will be delighted. Or frightened.

5. Sounds like a sidebar . . .

6. It *is* a sidebar!

**LETTER 5 Multipurpose Monster (Don't Try This at Home . . .)**

Greg Marr
Editor
*Silent Sports*
717 10th Street
P.O. Box 152
Waupaca, WI 54981

Mr. Marr:

① Here's the follow-up information you requested about the Buckshot Run and the Greenwood bike race.

The Buckshot Run is held on the Saturday of Labor Day weekend. There have been over 1,000 participants for the last three years. All proceeds go to support Indianhead Special Olympics.

② Past winners include Dan Conway, Dick Beardsley, and Dan Held, who holds the course record.

What's special about the race? It's very well organized, with support from many local firms and organizations, including the Indianhead Track Club. There are two distances, 2 and 5 miles. Runners are led to the starting lines of both races by a live marching band. (As opposed to a dead one, I suppose.) The race is actually a day-long event of sorts, with free food available to participants and

*(Continued)*

their families at two local downtown establishments after the actual running of the race.

(3)

As far as back-of-the-pack folks are concerned, this is a great run. It has become a real community event, with its namesake, local sportswriter Ron Buckli, serving as starter. Race founder Bob Lesniewski says that for many folks, this is their only race of the year. He adds that many friendly neighborhood rivalries are renewed each year, and that a lot of residents invite friends from Minnesota and surrounding areas, centering their weekend around the race. "The majority of our runners aren't concerned about picking up hardware, but about having a good time with their friends and neighbors," Bob says.

The bike race in Greenwood is a 30 miler that takes place on July 30. It's in its fifth year, and last year nearly 300 people took part. Race organizer Cheryl Lenz says that of those, at least one third were "tourers." (3)

(4)

The course is excellent for touring, with some gentle hills and quite a bit of flat. It passes through the countryside and past several Amish residences. I remember seeing a group of about fifteen Amish children during last year's race. It was a picturesque contrast, with the multicolored peloton flying past these children as they watched us solemnly in their bonnets, straw hats, and dark clothes.

*(Continued)*

⑤ The race was formerly held during Dairy Days. It is now held in conjunction with a large craft fair, and perhaps even better yet, a food fest. Several tables and a large tent are set up, and local groups sell fruit pizzas, cheese products, hamburgers, ice cream, etc. Just the thing to refuel the old bod. Ms. Lenz says that they plan to have either a band or a DJ this year, so that there will be musical entertainment for those waiting for the racers to return.

⑥ As I mentioned, I can get some course comments from the men's and women's winners, as well as the third place male finisher.

⑦ Two more local bicycling events have come to mind. One is the "Beat the Bugs" ride in May, sponsored yearly by the local chapter of a head injury club. It's a nice early season chance to do a group ride on a nice course, and usually attracts a good crowd, as well as some local television coverage. I know both hard core racers and back-of-the-pack folks who enjoy this one every year. Food stops are provided, the course goes through rolling farmland, and the sponsoring group really ties in well with educating the public about the importance of helmet use.

*(Continued)*

(7) I rode the Kiwanis Century in Chippewa Falls last year and enjoyed it. I talked to organizer Steve Thaler this week, and he says you covered the race last year, and that he has met you. I've got information about this year's race, so I can write that up as well, if you wish.

(8) Enough. I hope I'm not burying you in suggestions.
(9) I am eager to write what I can for you, however, so I look forward to your reply.

Sincerely,
Mike Perry

(10) P.S. I interviewed Dave Cihasky this week, and I've finished the rough draft of the article, so I should be able to send it to you soon.

## Comments, Letter 5

Please don't count the number of rules I broke with this letter. Just use it as an illustration of the observation I made earlier: Sometimes you must let yourself be guided by intuition. This editor had already given me one assignment and expressed an interest in two others. Make hay while the sun shines, my farmer forebears always said. Don't be fooled, however, into thinking you can make a practice of this sort of deluge.

1. The letter begins as a follow-up to a previous query. Marr had expressed interest in two stories, but wanted more information. No need to compose any fancy "grabber."

2. However, even though I was in follow-up mode, I had to remember: I was still in "sell" mode. Thus the mention of three "names" nationally recognized in running circles.

3. A specific reference to *Silent Sports* guidelines, which stipulate very strongly that the magazine may occasionally focus on big names or events, but must always remain loyal to the most of us who struggle along behind the leaders.

4. I hoped this scene would take the description of the route beyond distance and topography; when I wrote the piece, the scene was included.

5. Again, I knew that Marr was interested in pieces that go beyond the central event. I'm not sure why I used the phrase, "refuel the old bod."

6. This was in reference to previous correspondence regarding winners from the previous year. An example of offering inside information. Heck, even back-of-the-packers like to hear the secrets of the winners.

7. And now, in the category of "As Long as I'm at It. . . ." I ended up being assigned a piece on "Beat the Bugs."

8. Really.

9. Sounds overeager? It was true. And Mr. Marr gave me many of my first assignments of any length.

10. Doesn't hurt to mention that you haven't forgotten your original assignment.

A final comment: In this case, I knew that one editor handled all queries for *Silent Sports*. This isn't always the case. As a result, unless you have a firm grasp on the division of editorial responsibilities, it's rarely a good idea to pitch more than one idea per query, as different editors within the same magazine handle different topics. Why risk losing a chance to pitch idea number two just because it's attached to idea number one and never got forwarded to the proper person?

**LETTER 6 Query/Cover Letter**

Craig Renner
Culture Editor
*The World & I*
3600 New York Avenue, N.E.
Washington, DC 20002

Mr. Renner:

(1) Do you remember where you were the day Big Boy died? The news came out of Toledo, and it wasn't pretty. Big Boy: ripped from his feet, beheaded and chunked, and the bits tossed around town. (2) An entire nation reacted with dismay (and took time out from O.J. to do so).

(3) But why?

Because America is fascinated by big things. From the (5) Jolly Green Giant to (4) 9,000-pound prairie chickens in love, from Mt. Rushmore to Paul Bunyan, big has always attracted our attention. The F.A.S.T. corporation in Sparta, Wisconsin, even goes so far as to refer to its outsized products as "people attractors." (4)

*(Continued)*

I wrote the enclosed (unpublished) piece upon hearing of Big Boy's demise, and am submitting it as a form of proposal. If you are interested in the topic, I would like to (6) tailor and update the piece to further address the cultural significance of "Big Things" in America.

Thank you for your time and attention. I look forward to your reply.

Sincerely,
Michael Perry

## Comments, Letter 6

As you can tell by reading it, this letter accompanied an unsolicited manuscript. The manuscript led off with three epigraphs and a lengthy introductory setup. Thus, it ran the risk of being discarded before the editor reached the crux of the story. And so I included the cover letter as a sort of preliminary synopsis.

1. An official "grabber."

2. I was pitching the culture editor. How's that for cultural context?

3. The aforementioned crux.

4,5. By citing the absurd and relatively unknown (4) in contrast with the absurd and relatively well known (5), I'm trying to cast the piece as offbeat but relevant.

6. The piece was not originally written for *The World & I,* and required some adjustment if accepted; it's important to let an editor know you are aware and willing.

**LETTER 7 Cover Letter Accompanying an Unsolicited Essay**

Editor
*Orion*
136 East 64th Street
New York, NY 10021

① Enclosed please find an essay that addresses the trend toward what has been termed "Look at Me" architecture, in which the landscape is subverted in order to serve as a display case for ego-puffing abodes.

② My publishing credits include essays and nonfiction pieces for a number of publications ranging from *Newsweek* to *The Christian Science Monitor* to *The World & I*.

Thank you for your time and consideration. I look forward to your reply.

Sincerely,
Michael Perry

③ *limited simultaneous submission*

## Comments, Letter 7

This letter accompanied an unsolicited essay. I don't believe it is wise to submit an essay without a brief explanation. Before an editor will be interested in the take, he or she will want to know if the topic is a match with his or her publication.

1. Essay in a nutshell.
2. "Street credentials." Abbreviated boasting.
3. If you're submitting it more than one place at once, say so.

**LETTER 8 Variation on a Letter Accompanying an Unsolicited Essay**

Rick Herrick
Editor
*Quality Living*
Post Office Box One
Valle Crucis, NC 28691

Dear Mr. Herrick:

① Thank you for the check for my essay, "Lesson in the Rain." I look forward to my sample copies. ② It was an honor to contribute to your magazine.

③ I have enclosed another essay for your consideration. The seeds for this piece were planted over many years, but they really came to bloom one day in Norway, as you will see.

③ While the essay reflects my true feelings about a topic that niggles me, I have attempted to use a little humor to make my point. ④ I hope this is not interpreted as cynicism, which your writer's guidelines indicate you are not interested in. (A famous writer once said, "I have never scoffed at sentiment. Cynicism is ever the outward face of emptiness," and I agree. In some cases, cynicism has the same essential tempering qualities as realism. However, to wallow in it, and to dismiss hope and optimism with a scornful sneer, is perhaps the most

*(Continued)*

④ cowardly of actions; anyone can come to see what a horrible place the world is. It takes someone with courage to seek out some good, to dare to pursue a romantic vision in that same world.)

⑤ But I digress. (Do I ever!)

Sincerely,
Michael Perry

⑥ P.S. The piece is stored on disk, so there is no need to return the manuscript.

## Comments, Letter 8

1. Don't assume an editor remembers who you are. Saying thanks instead of "remember me?" seemed a classier means of accomplishing that end.

2. Well . . . I *was* pleased, but in retrospect, "honor" seems a bit grandiose.

3. The editor did eventually purchase this essay. However, as far as I'm concerned, I missed the boat in the next two paragraphs. *I never describe the topic of the essay.* There's no reason for any of my rambling from here on. I can tell I didn't intend to "tease," but that's what it amounts to, and trust me, editors are not amused by this sort of thing.

4. I will offer one bit of defense for all of this indefensible rambling: I wanted to be sure the editor knew I wasn't ignoring the publication's guidelines.

5. Silly, weak, and cutesy to death. Makes me cringe. Can't believe I wrote it. I hope we've both learned something.

6. Important note if you haven't included sufficient postage to return the manuscript.

**LETTER 9 Cover Letter Accompanying an Unsolicited Humor Piece**

Suzanne Frey
Editor
*The Toastmaster*
P.O. Box 9052
Mission Viejo, CA 92690-7052

Ms. Frey:

Enclosed for your consideration is a humorous essay on how one contemporary male is dealing with impending baldness.

From sorting through ubiquitous hair-loss infomercials to choosing a baldness support group, "Hirsute Pursuits" addresses every balding man's concerns.

Thank you for your time and consideration. I look forward to your reply.

Sincerely,
Michael Perry

*limited simultaneous submission*

## Comments, Letter 9

Two short paragraphs. The editor will still have to read the piece to discover if the piece really is humorous (I should have used the word "humor," not "humorous"), but he or she can tell if the topic is relevant.

## IF THEY SAY YES

In the previous chapter, we talked abut how to handle rejection. But how should you handle acceptance?

- First of all, I never consider an article sold or published until the check is in the bank and the magazine is on the rack. The first article I ever had accepted by a magazine appeared in that magazine only after a couple years and a flotilla of editors came and went. What I thought would be my first published work never hit print until long after I'd stopped keeping track of firsts.
- Before you agree to do a piece, ask if you will be assigned a kill fee. A kill fee is the amount of money a publication pays the writer for a piece that is assigned but subsequently cancelled.
- Know what rights you will be selling (see Chapter 13).
- Understand that if you agree to write a piece "on spec," the editor has only agreed to look at—not necessarily purchase—the piece when it is finished.
- It is a good practice to get a contract or letter of acceptance in writing. The only reason I don't say "always" is because I've produced a number of pieces over the years under much more informal circumstances. Frankly, this is both a reality and a bad idea.

CHAPTER

NINE

# How to Be an Expert on Everything

If you're trying to sell an article to an editor, it never hurts to dangle the promise of "inside information." But before you can get inside information . . . well . . . you have to get *inside.* The good news is, assuming we're not talking about a six-part series detailing life in the Mob, getting inside (and back out alive) isn't that tough. Follow a few guidelines, follow your instincts, follow your nose, and you'll locate those sources of inside information that allow you to go beyond writing material that simply informs readers to writing material that makes readers feel as if they are being given privileged access; as if they are being personally put "in the know."

## WHERE DO I BEGIN?

First, let's talk briefly about *when* to begin. In most cases, you'll need to dig up a little inside information just to put your article proposal together. You'll need to give an editor the specific details of where your information will be coming from; how, where, and from whom you will be obtaining it. You may need to conduct a few preliminary interviews, do a little preliminary research. In other cases it will be enough to simply indicate where you *intend* to get your information. A brief list of potential sources will suffice. A word of caution: don't promise the moon unless you possess a ticket to that particular dusty sphere. If you sell an article to an editor on the premise that you're an expert on paleontology, and then, come crunch time, are forced to admit that your paleontological preparation amounts to a repeat rental of *Jurassic Park,* well, obviously you're about to be party to the extinction of your assignment. Don't tell an editor you intend to quote classified Pentagon papers unless you've got them in your paws (and, I suppose, are willing to go to the Big House). On the same principle—and I'll elaborate on this in Chapter Ten—don't promise an editor that you intend to enlist the services of both the Surgeon General and Tommy Lasorda as consulting experts on a piece examining the impact of chewing tobacco on the ability of major league pitchers to get dates unless you have the phone numbers of, and an appointment with, both individuals.

Now then. Where to begin.

An organized approach is nice. Actually, it's more than "nice." Streamline the process wherever you can and your work-to-pay ratio will be more profitable. But I say it's "nice" simply to infer that—at least in my case—organization tends to give way to curiosity. One of my great weaknesses in the research process is my distractibility. I'll be researching a piece on principles of oxygenation when I come across a story about vintage Cadillac ambulances, and the next thing I know, twenty minutes have passed and I've done nothing more than a little recreational reading. So I'll get back on track, until I come across a fascinating piece on how to achieve cervical stabilization through the application of a blanket rolled in the shape of a horse collar. Another ten minutes shot. And so on. *Stay* on task, don't *stray* on task. There. I've invented an aphorism for the occasion. I hope it helps you more than it helps me.

One way to organize the search for information is to apply a corollary of newspaper journalism's inverted pyramid theory. That is, organize your research so that you begin with the broad end of your topic and then proceed to the specifics. Apply this method, and your progression is likely to be smoother. I find this to be especially true when I do medical pieces. For instance, I recently completed a textbook chapter on the general topic of trauma. Contrary to my usual procedure, I did a computer search of professional journals before I did a computer search of textbooks. As a result, I wasted some time early on piecing together topics from bits of information gleaned from an article here and an article there; when I got around to looking at the textbooks, of course I found them to be much more broadly definitive. The topics I was piecing together were already pieced together for me. Based on past experience, I knew better, but I got my nose so deep into the material that I had to look at a passel of trees before I realized my time would be better spent backing off for a look at the forest.

As nice as an organized approach is, it has been my experience (and thus, may simply be a reflection of my predilection to disorganization) that at some point the process of gathering information for a story becomes intuitive and tangential. One source suggests another, a lead forks and you follow both angles, you explore a connection based on a hunch. As long as you're not completely off track (i.e., reading stories about vintage Cadillac ambulances) and involved in wholesale time wastage, I think this is fine. When I am writing creative nonfiction, I find the pursuit of tangents and intuition to be invaluable. It is on these meanders that a writer often discovers those connections or juxtapositions that lend a sense of revelation to a piece. In some cases, these pursuits lead to an idea for another piece. You are a writer, and even when you're off track, you should be snuffling around for anything you suspect to be of use.

When I am composing didactic text for a chapter on techniques of surgical repair for acute ruptures of the patellar tendon, on the other hand, tangents and intuition (*especially* intuition) are not only time-wasters, they are potential ground for professional censure and loss of writing privileges!

## EXPERT SOURCES

And so where should this search for expert information be directed? In *The Complete Guide to Magazine Article Writing,* John M. Wilson suggests that you begin the search by asking yourself the following question: *Who would know?* It's a simple, understated, and excellent recommendation.

So. With John Wilson's question as a starting point, a selection of destinations follows.

### Librarians

For my money, librarians are one of the most overlooked sources of expert information. Reference librarians are professional information hunters. I deserve a swift kick in the shorts for all the times I've stubbornly wound my way through the library stacks, my mule head leading the way, searching fruitlessly for information a librarian could put in my hands in a matter of minutes. Librarians not only know what's in the library and where to find it, they know what's *not* in the library and where to find it. Librarians are also an excellent source of pertinent tangents. I've been sent down many an unanticipated but productive path by a librarian who said, "Maybe you should consider looking under. . . ." Finally, not only is it a librarian's job to assist you in your search, most of them enjoy it thoroughly. The best are tenacious informational gumshoes, happiest when they are on the case.

And don't forget: You don't necessarily have to go to the library to be helped by a librarian. I've been assisted by librarians on a number of projects over the phone. If your research does require you to actually go to the library, an advance call to the librarian may streamline your efforts once you arrive. The librarian will probably appreciate the chance to get some preliminary work done without you looking over his shoulder and tapping your foot.

## The Yellow Pages

Need a quote for an article on lawn care? Head for the Yellow Pages, look under lawn maintenance. Putting together a piece on what it takes to get a black belt? Try the Yellow Pages; "Kung Fu Instruction" ought to do it. Need something more than your local Yellow Pages? Most decent-sized libraries have comprehensive phone book holdings that include all the major metropolitan areas in the United States. And a number of on-line services offer access to national compilations of Yellow Pages and other business listings.

## Specialized Groups

Whether you be a lawyer, a ballerina, the owner of a Studebaker, or victim—as are David Letterman, Lauren Hutton, Maya Angelou, Jerry Falwell, and I—of a diastema (a gap between two teeth), there's a group for you. In case of Dave, Maya, and I, it's the International Diastema Club. These groups are excellent sources of expert—or at least "inside"—information. And don't simply think in terms of *people*—whether it be hobbies, industry, theory, worship, or you name it, associations are formed on the basis of virtually any similarity you can conjure. For the article on water towers I've mentioned previously, I obtained useful information from the Steel Plate Fabricators Association; I was also assisted by members of an association devoted strictly to popular culture. Where do you find these folks? The commonly available *Encyclopedia of Associations* is a good bet; it is described as "listing more than 22,000 active associations, organizations, clubs and other non-profit membership groups in a variety of fields." Can't find it there? Read on.

## Specialized Directories and Indexes

Take a stroll through the reference section of a decent-sized library, and it may seem that specialized directories are nearly as ubiquitous and diverse as the groups and information they list. From the obvious—phone numbers, associations—to the obscure—arcane experts, regional medical authorities—directories are an excellent source of sources. Just as there is an association for everyone, there's a directory for everyone . . . as *The Directory of Directories* proves!

Think tangentially when you're searching directories. For instance, if the topic you're researching isn't represented by an association, perhaps it is represented by common literature, in which case you might locate the information you're after via the *Oxbridge Directory of Newsletters,* which lists over 20,000 newsletters, loose-leaf publications, bulletins, and fax letters.

### Expert Experts

*Dial-an-Expert* is a directory listing "nearly 700 national experts on topics ranging from abortion to writing." ProfNet is a service linking 2,700 public information officers by Internet; writers can submit queries by phone, fax, e-mail, or snail mail and with any luck, receive an expert reply—all for no charge. Directories and services like these can be valuable tools for the writer, but keep a few points in mind:

- Don't become part of an advertising campaign. Is the "expert" truly an expert, or is he or she a publicist or public relations person?

Nothing says you can't obtain useful information from a publicist (and as John M. Wilson points out in *The Complete Guide to Magazine Article Writing,* they can help you with fact-checking and background information), but never forget that these folks are paid to promote and protect a specific set of interests.

• Just because an expert isn't employed in public relations doesn't mean that expert isn't pushing an agenda. Pay attention to what the person is saying; is a second, balancing opinion necessary? The last thing you want to do is serve as an unwitting flack for someone's pet theory, project, or peeve. If you know disagreement or controversy exists, ask about it. The way an individual responds to a conflicting opinion is far more revealing than the opinion he espouses unopposed.

• Whenever possible, don't settle for a single expert source. Beyond addressing concerns of balance, comments from a selection of sources will provide your readers with greater depth and a richer perspective.

• Finally, although it is tempting—in the interest of expediency—to seek out conveniently listed experts, keep in mind that the most easily accessible experts are also likely to be the most frequently quoted. There's nothing necessarily wrong with that, especially if the individual is truly the established leader in her field, but to paraphrase Gary Stern, author of "How to Become an Instant Expert," in *1,082 Tips to Write Better and Sell More,* lesser-known sources will bring new voices—and a sense of freshness—to your work.

## Federal, State, and City Government

Based on my experience writing a piece on copyright and trademark for *Business* magazine, the federal government is an excellent source of information if you are blessed with an infinite store of patience. By now we are all familiar with the endless loops of automated phone systems; if ever there was a technology custom-made for bureaucrats, this is it. It's a form of progress: Rather than stand in line at some grey government building, you now stand in line on the line. I did get good information in the end, but I still haven't got the crick out of my neck. I obtained much of my information (and you can, too) through the

Superintendent of Documents, at the General Printing Office, Washington, DC 20242. Specialty publications including the *Monthly Catalog of U.S. Government Publications* provide another avenue of pursuit. A call to the nearest university may also be productive; a certain number of university libraries across the country maintain repositories of government documents.

Don't overlook government-sponsored information sources available closer to home. For instance, if I were to do an article about the effects of zebra mussels on Wisconsin's waterways, I'd be sure to check in with the state Department of Natural Resources. And when I was developing a piece for the local chamber of commerce, I received helpful information from several local city government sources.

## Newspaper Reporters

While working on regional topics, I've often made use of contacts in the newspaper business. The reporter isn't likely to be expert, but *is* likely to have a pretty good idea where to send you. After all, these folks spend much of their time tracking down someone who can give a definitive statement on the topic of the day.

## Corporate Libraries and Archives

A surprising number of businesses and institutions maintain specialized libraries, archives, or both. Over the years, I've turned to the library of a leading computer manufacturer, a law office library, a number of hospital libraries, newspaper archives, university libraries and archives, and even the archives of a company that built bridges. Corporate libraries are a fantastic source of extensive, in-depth information on "niche" topics. Because they focus on specific subject areas, corporate libraries are able to devote their resources to assembling much more comprehensive holdings on a particular topic than public libraries. The information is updated regularly to maintain a pace with the rest of the industry. Some of the information you won't necessarily find in a public library includes:

**Unlisted or Obscure Trade Journals.** An excellent source of up-to-the-minute expert information.

**Textbooks.** While textbooks are more quickly dated than trade journals, they are excellent resources for general overview information, especially if you are writing about an area you may not be intimately familiar with. With their teaching prose and accompanying glossaries, textbooks can lay the foundation for your piece.

**Definitive Works.** Nearly every subject area has its "classics," written works that define the topic itself and set the standard against which all subsequent works will be measured. These include groundbreaking research pieces, subject-specific dictionaries, and touchstone texts. Most corporate libraries will have these works on hand, and they will be invaluable to the writer familiarizing himself or herself with a new topic.

**Specialized Searches.** When it comes to specific, narrow-topic research, corporate libraries are often superior to public libraries. A corporate librarian is likely to be aware of specialized indexes and directories. In addition to indexes and directories in printed form, most corporate libraries now have computerized search capabilities.

If the corporate library you are using does not have the material you need on hand, chances are good the librarian can obtain it for you, or direct you to it. Most corporate libraries have access to interlibrary loan programs similar to those used by public libraries—so your search need not be limited by local resources.

A few more notes about corporate libraries:

**Access.** Access to corporate libraries varies. Some are open to the public, while others are restricted to employee use only. In most cases, a brief phone call is all that is necessary to find out if the library is open to the public. In other cases, a polite letter stating your background and purpose for wishing to use the library will do the trick.

Anyone who has been writing for a while is aware that "no" isn't always the final word. If you are tactful, polite, and blessed with a little good fortune, you will find a way to get into even those libraries with restricted access. And in the "not what you know, but whom you know" department, a friend who has access might be able to obtain the permission you need to get in the door.

**Usage Fees.** Most libraries charge a nominal fee for searches. These rates vary from institution to institution, and if similar libraries exist within close range, I have found that it pays to shop around. One hospital library I use for the majority of my research does not charge for on-line time; its counterpart—located in the same town—does.

**Locating Corporate Libraries in Your Area.** Some corporate libraries are included in the American Library Association listings (available at your local public library); most are not. The librarian at your local public library will often be aware of corporate libraries in the area, and can provide a referral.

Of course, if you are interested in information unique to a particular industry or discipline, a quick glance through the business section of your phone book will provide you with a list of numbers to try.

When you're doing research in a corporate library, recall our earlier discussion and don't overlook the most valuable resource at your disposal: the librarian! Just like the collections they maintain, corporate librarians possess specialized knowledge. The librarian will be able to direct and assist you in your search, eliminating the wasted time that comes from bulling your way through an unfamiliar system on your own.

## Finding Stories and Work in Professional Journals

While you're researching your story in a library with special holdings, don't forget to keep your radar active for other story ideas. Professional journals are an excellent source of breaking developments that the general media have often not picked up on. For instance, the *New England Journal of Medicine* is frequently the source of breaking medical stories. By reviewing these specialized publications regularly, you can learn to spot trends that when converted to layperson's terms and applied to everyday life will produce the type of timely articles editors everywhere hunger for.

Many journals are not included in popular market listings. As a result, their editors are not inundated with queries and proposals, and your chances for publication are improved. On the other hand, their specificity often demands an in-depth knowledge and familiarity with the subject matter. However, by glancing through their contents you will be able to judge for yourself the likelihood of your being able to contribute, and you will discover that many of these publications do accept material of a more general nature.

## FINDING "UNKNOWN" EXPERTS IN PRINT

Assume for the moment that you wish to submit a proposal to a national health magazine on recent advances in treatments of fractures of the calcaneus. In order to make your proposal more tempting, you wish to indicate that you have access to leading authorities in the field. Since most people don't even know what a calcaneus is (it's your heel bone, by the way), it is likely that national experts on the subject are relatively obscure.

No problem. A quick search of the literature will yield several journal articles and textbook titles. These articles and textbooks, in turn, will yield the names and often the addresses of the experts who wrote them. In most cases, a polite letter will yield a productive interview with an expert happy to share information about her specialty—as a matter of fact, the more obscure the information, the more likely she will be interested in sharing it!

In research publications, the names and addresses of the researchers are commonly published at the end of each piece. If not, the journal editor will generally be more than happy to help you reach the party in question. If privacy is an issue, you may have to send your request to the editor, who will then forward it to the individual in question.

Textbooks normally include the addresses of contributing editors, also. For those whose address is not printed, it has been my experience that the publishers themselves are usually very willing to assist me in making contact with authors once I state my purpose.

## CYBERSEARCHING

The Internet is a fascinating source of information. I use it all the time. But you must be judicious, and you must be cautious. Anyone can post anything on the World Wide Web. Do you know for sure that treatise on mule skinning by Professor Garibaldi Persimmon is the real deal?

Or did someone concoct it for kicks, in the hopes that another someone compiling a history of 19th-century animal rendering procedures would unwittingly use it to flesh out a cover story for *Frontier Life Monthly*?

There are a number of different ways to perform cybersearches. You might be working through a general service the likes of Compuserve or America Online, or perhaps you're a subscriber to a small local Internet provider, in which case you'll probably rely on a topical search engine the likes of Excite, InfoSeek, or Yahoo. Be aware that the results of your search will be directly affected by the quirks of the system you use. Search engines are idiosyncratic, and set up to scan for different things in different ways. Search tips are usually provided, and they're worth a read. The narrower the search parameters you set, the better your odds of striking usable material. That said, however, if you are unfamiliar with the subject you are researching, a broad search will likely (eventually) lead to the information you require.

Because it is so easy to search, and because it can deliver reams and reams of information from all over the world directly into your writer's garret, it is also easy to fall into the trap of limiting your research to cyberspace. Big mistake. Just because a search using the keywords "water tower" yields 4,587 "hits," don't assume the search was definitive. You still need to do your off-line (library) research and talk to real people. When it comes to topical information floating out there in cyberspace, sheer volume shouldn't be confused with comprehensiveness.

## The Great Thing About Experts

The great thing about experts, beyond the fact that they are the experts, is that the majority of them are great interviewees. The very fact that someone is considered an expert in an area reflects his or her passion in that area, and as a result, most experts passionately desire to talk about that specialty. They also tend to try to prove their expert status by saying things like, "now most people don't realize this about water towers, but. . .," at which point they divulge just the sort of nugget that will ratchet the interest level of your piece up another notch. In some cases, experts toil in obscurity for years, deprived of recognition for their efforts, and they see an interview as their one chance to show the world what they've been doing all that time.

The other great thing about experts is their familiarity with *other* experts. Never end an "expert" interview without asking the question, "Is there anyone else I should talk to about this topic?" In all but the most egotistical cases, you'll come away with a lead or two.

One thing you must remember when interviewing an expert is that when it comes time to write your finished piece, you'll have to convey the expert's information to a general readership in an understandable form. Beware jargon, lingo, and overly technical references. If esoteric references crop up, make sure you understand them; ask the expert to clarify when necessary. Also make sure you can provide a lay translation of any technical terms. The expert is often very helpful in this regard.

## Not All Experts Reside in Ivory Towers

I once viewed a fascinating (one former farmboy's opinion) documentary in which professors of agriculture and agronomists and Ph.D. candidates explained the intricacies of manure and its distribution, including fascinating new manure-spreading techniques that relied on global positioning satellite technology to distribute the "material" evenly. Now then. Were I to be assigned a piece on advances in manure-spreading methods, I'd look these folks up. After all, in an esoteric (and aromatic) field, they are the experts. But I'd also have a chat with my brother. He's a farmer, you see, and his manure-spreading technology comes with tines and a wooden handle. And as I recall from my childhood, no understanding of the intricacies of manure and its distribution are complete without a little time spent running a pitchfork.

As Gary Stern points out, experts may be "removed from the action," and their theories may not be compatible with reality. And so, my point is this: Don't quote the generals without giving some consideration to the folks out on the front lines. (Or front tines.)

## Keep an Expert Eye Out

Just because you don't need an expert now, doesn't mean you won't need one later. In *1,082 Tips to Write Better and Sell More,* Gary Stern writes:

> I make note of experts I see quoted in leading newspapers and magazines. . . . You never know when you'll land an assignment that will allow you to make use of such sources.

He's right.

I once read a profile of renowned landscape architect Dan Kiley in *The New Yorker.* I know nothing about landscape architecture, but I filed the name away. A year or so later, I was working on an essay about people who build their houses atop hills for all the world to see. Essentially, the piece amounted to little more than my amateur grumbling on the subject. And so, on a whim, I dug up the reference to Mr. Kiley, tracked down his address, and sent him a letter posing a few brief questions on the topic. He responded in a terse, eloquent, and relevant paragraph. It was just the touch the essay needed. My essay was subsequently published in *Orion* magazine; I am confident that without Mr. Kiley's comments, the piece would have been much more difficult to place.

## GIVE THANKS

Keep track of the folks who help you. Send a note of thanks their way when the project is completed, or express your appreciation with a phone call. It's not just good manners, it's a good idea; you never know when you'll need their help again.

Also, whenever possible and realistic, I send those who help me get the goods a copy of the published piece. If the number of people I contacted was such that this isn't realistic, I still try to let them know when and where the piece appeared, and how they might obtain a copy.

### REMEMBER . . .

While you're rummaging around in search of inside information—and especially when you're doing research in libraries or archives with specialized collections—remember what we discussed in Chapter Six: Beyond your current project, keep your eyes open for future projects. Notice any new professional journals? Any you might be suited to write for? Scan tables of contents: See anything that might apply to a broader audience? A trend, a breaking development, something the mainstream media may not yet have picked up on? Something you can package in a timely story for a hungry editor somewhere?

## YOU, YOURSELF

While you're running hither and yon in search of experts, don't forget to look in the mirror. You can talk to all the experts you can track down, but in the end, your readers are relying on you to deliver the big picture. When I did the previously referenced article on monster trucks, I talked to the obvious experts, from the man who designed the first monster truck to the top two drivers on the national championship circuit. But I also crawled into the cab of Big Foot,® and took exhaustive, detailed notes of everything I could see. I jotted notes about how it felt to be strapped in, what all the gauges said, how they were arranged, how the accelerator pedal differed from the ones in our cars, what the view over the hood was like, how the roll bars were arranged overhead, what the graffiti on the cab walls said. When I climbed down, I had several legal pad pages filled with notes. Why? Because I knew that part of my responsibility within the article would be to take lay readers as far into the experience of driving a monster truck as possible without actually giving them the keys. And so, within the constraints of time (three days in Indianapolis) and safety (I didn't get to smash any cars—*rats*!), I had a responsibility to those readers to immerse myself in the topic as completely as possible. When the reader finds himself sitting at the starting line, gripping the wheel attached to 10,000 pounds of raging monster truck, in a sense I am cast in the role of expert, describing the experience from a position of knowledge rather than speculation.

I don't mean to intimate that a weekend spent hanging out at a race track, coupled with a fifteen-minute sit in a monster truck, makes me an expert on the subject. I'm simply trying to reinforce the fact that as a writer, you will find yourself called upon to make deeply descriptive, definitive statements on topics you have been completely unfamiliar with a week previously, and as such, you must do everything you can in the time you have to arm yourself with information and observation unavailable to the average person on the street.

# CHAPTER TEN

# THE HORSE'S MOUTH: INTERVIEWING

Interviewing is an art. It's knowing what to ask, how to ask, and when to ask. It's knowing when to ask nothing at all. It's knowing when to step in and redirect the exchange, and it's knowing when to run with a tangent. You must establish a rapport with your subject. You must frame your questions in such a way that the information you elicit is fresh. You attempt to put the subject at ease, take your source to that emotional place where he or she feels free to share, to speak freely.

An example: A few years ago, I interviewed over-the-top, meat-eating, guitar-and-arrow-slinging rocker Ted "Deadly Tedly" Nugent, also known as The Motor City Madman. I prepared for the interview by diligently researching his career. I listened to his music. I boned up on the fact that he was a controversial pro-hunting figure in the mostly anti-hunting music industry. I discovered that his wife's name was Shemane. Based on this research and the principles I outlined in the opening paragraph, I prepared notes and questions. When my telephone rang, I was well prepared. To demonstrate the payoffs of preparation, I offer a transcript summarizing my comments over the duration of the ensuing 15-minute interview:

"Hello."

"Oh, well thanks for taking the ti . . ."

"Uh-huh."

"Yeah."

"Uh-huh."

"Mmm."

(Repeat above sequence for 15 minutes.)

And finally,

"Yes, well you keep rocking, too, Mr. Nugent."

Somewhere, I still have a tape of that interview. And someday, perhaps when Ted is on the Rocked-Out Rest Home Revival Tour, I'll dig it out and have a listen. But I expect I'll be just as embarrassed then as I was when I played the thing back the first time. Ted comes off as an articulate, bombastic, hyperkinetic, polysyllabic rock star with his throttle stuck in the "rabbit" position. I come off as a grinning idiot.

Welcome to the fine art of interviewing.

## OBTAINING THE INTERVIEW

Interviews generally begin with a "cold call," either to the person to be interviewed or that person's handlers. I was loath to make my first cold call, I was loath to make my most recent, and I was loath to make every one in between. Try as I might, despite the fact that things usually work out just fine, I haven't found a way to make cold calling fun.

But unless you can make a living composing essays off the top of your head, interviews are a part of the freelance life, and cold calls are a part of interviewing. So we'll dispense with the whining and shuddering and move on.

The process of obtaining an interview will vary with circumstance. In some cases, a single phone call does it all. In other cases, the process unfolds over several months, several calls, a letter here and there, and a series of negotiations roughly equivalent to the structuring of a nuclear test ban agreement between superpowers. In *The Complete Guide to Magazine Article Writing,* John M. Wilson likens the process to going through layers of insulation, with the layers increasing, "the higher the person's position or the greater his success or fame."

If your subject is a celebrity, you'll probably do your preliminary dealings with a publicist or personal manager. A tip: You'll sometimes have a bit more luck with a production publicist (a person promoting a *project*) than a personal publicist (the person reporting directly to the individual you hope to interview), as the production publicist has a vested interest in giving you access, while the personal publicist may be more concerned with maintaining your potential subject's privacy.

It has been my experience that a publicist (usually with a management company) serves as the primary filter, relaying your request, checking on availability, checking up on you and the publication you're writing for. After the initial request is approved, you'll probably deal with the subject's personal manager immediately before, during, and after the interview. As in any business, there's plenty of room for miscommunication; make sure you take notes and names throughout "negotiations"; I've shown up for interviews only to meet a personal manager who never heard of me. In that case, I simply give the name of the individual I had been dealing with to set up the meeting. At that point, someone usually produces a cel phone, a call is made, and before long, the interview is underway.

## The Interview Catch-22

Which came first? The interview or the assignment?

To land an interview with an individual of prominence, you'll need credence, generally in the form of an assignment. On the other hand, one of the ways you get that assignment is by assuring an editor that you can deliver that interview.

In some cases (if the individual in question is on a quest to publicize a current project, for instance), you may be able to obtain a commitment for an interview contingent on your procuring an assignment. But in most cases, you'll need to convince an editor to assign you the story before you have any chance of convincing the individual of prominence to sit for an interview. Ultimately, you'll need to establish a track record. Over the years, I've developed a sort of country music subspecialty. I never make guarantees I can't back up, but if I come to an editor with a decent story idea involving a country performer, that editor can look at my clips and resume and see that I understand how the machinery works and have as good a chance as anyone to lock up an interview.

Let me reinforce: Do not promise an interview you can't deliver. Don't use a big name to get an assignment and then destroy your credibility when you fall on your face and fail to get access. If I have any doubt, I tell the editor, "Here's my story idea involving Individual X; if you think the story will work for you, give me a written commitment and the go-ahead to start the wheels turning. If I can get the interview, we'll work from there."

## THE PREEMPTIVE LETTER

If I get an assignment requiring me to interview a celebrity, or someone who won't necessarily swing the door wide open when I knock, I ask the editor to send me a letter on the magazine's letterhead confirming the magazine's commitment to the story and stating clearly that I am the writer assigned to the piece. You might call it a letter of introduction.

When I got an assignment, for example, to write a piece about country music performer Aaron Tippin and his gun shop, the editor of *Heartland USA* sent me a letter reading as follows:

> This is to confirm our interest in the story on Aaron Tippin's gun shop you queried us about recently. As we discussed on the phone, we're always looking for a different angle to take when profiling a celebrity. I'm convinced our readership—country fans (and gun enthusiasts) almost to a person—will enjoy learning about this other side of Tippin.
>
> Looking forward to seeing the finished piece.

Once I had the letter in hand, I called Tippin's management company, *briefly* introduced myself, *briefly* described the magazine I was representing, *briefly* (and in general terms) explained the proposed focus of the story, and obtained the name of the appropriate contact person. I then faxed a typed copy of the request, a copy of my writing resume, and a copy of the editor's letter to that contact person.

I have duplicated this process on any number of stories.

In addition to the preemptive letter (John M. Wilson refers to it as a "letter of assignment"), be prepared to provide the name and number of your editor.

Also be prepared to explain what the general focus of the article will be, but don't make any promises. I recently encountered a situation in which a promotions director met my request for information by demanding to know what kind of "ink" his company was going to get, and what was "in it" for him. Because I needed information he had, I did the old soft-shoe until I got that information, but I made it *very* clear (in an understated, soft-shoe kind of way) that I wasn't about to promise him exposure in return for that information.

## FOLLOW-UP

In some cases, interviews are easily obtained. In other cases, polite persistence is necessary. A phone call a week following your request is reasonable; anything further requires case-to-case judgment.

## CONDUCTING THE INTERVIEW

The interview itself is a tough topic to address in an organized fashion, because there is no such thing as a typical interview. I've conducted interviews that lasted less than a minute, and I've been assigned projects that involved shadowing (basically an extended interview) someone for a month. I've done interviews over the phone, and I've done interviews from the copilot's seat of a stunt plane in flight. Rather than force information into false categories, I'll simply share what I've learned about interviews and interviewing, from preparation to execution.

### Be Prepared

The more you prepare for an interview, the more likely you are to get good material. Although you'll be forced to at times, "winging it" is never a good idea if you have time to prepare beforehand.

• Do your research. If your interview is topic-focused, study the topic. If your interview is personality-focused, study the person (more on this later in this section). I can't give you any set formula, but the amount of research you need to do is roughly proportional to the depth of the piece. If you're interviewing the president of a frozen pizza company for a 400-word news bit on a new dough roller, there's no need to review her high school yearbook. If, on the other hand, you're profiling the pizza exec for an in-depth cover story profile for a major business magazine, you'll want as much background information as you can get your hands on; in addition to the yearbook, you'll want to research frozen pizza trends and technology, the executive's educational and career path, in-depth biographical information, etc.

• Think about the nature of the piece you intend to write. Based on those thoughts, what information do you need from the person you will be interviewing? Personal information? Professional information? Hard data? Opinions?

• Compile a list of questions. There's no need to plod through your list, checking each question off as you ask it (see the "Conversing" section below). Once you get rolling, you can and will improvise questions, but don't rely on improvisation to get started or sustain the interview. Nothing will dampen your subject's spirit of cooperation like a stop-and-go interview salted throughout with "umm's" and "aah's." Odds are, if the person you are interviewing is important enough to interview, that person is too important to sit around waiting for you to get your ducks in a row.

• Order your list of questions by priority. Again, that doesn't mean you should plow through the list in order; you'll want to feel your way into the interview, establish a level of rapport with the subject, before you ask the big or tough questions. But you should have a good sense of those questions you most need answered to suit your piece.

• Check your list against your research. Don't waste your time or your subject's time asking for information available elsewhere. For instance, before I interview a musical artist, I review (at the very least) the artist's press pack, which is gladly supplied by the artist's management. Not only do these packs contain the basics—bio, career chronology, album titles, etc.—they frequently include a collection of previously published pieces. Read these pieces, for not only will they educate you about your subject, you'll get a sense for what's already been said to death and can avoid cranking out the same old thing. I also make sure I'm familiar with the artist's work, even if this means listening to a few album's worth of music I'd normally avoid.

Over the years, I've discovered that preinterview preparation provides another invaluable advantage, best described by quoting John M. Wilson:

> As you do your backgrounding, you'll not only gather material that will be used in the article itself, but you'll find your discoveries triggering questions you never would have thought to ask.

That has certainly been my experience. One rather fluffy example comes quickly to mind. Preparing to write a piece about a large country music festival for *Country Weekly* by grinding through a pile of the aforementioned press packs, I learned that the bass player in the country band The Mavericks was married to country singer Tricia Yearwood. Yearwood was following The Mavericks on the bill on one of the days I was covering the festival, and so I made sure to ask her husband about their unique situation. As it turned out, the couple had taken advantage of the rare opportunity to be together on the road by sneaking out to go antique shopping in a nearby town. The mini-reunion rated its own paragraph in the piece. Had I skipped the preparation, I would still have filed a story, but I would have missed a great little human interest angle.

## Go Beyond the Obvious

Spend a little time in the media tent at a country music festival and you learn a valuable lesson about the payoffs of preparation. Just prior to or just after performing, artists are escorted into the tent, placed in a plastic lawn chair, and subjected to what might best be described as an interview assembly line. The artist does one interview after the other, answering roughly the same five questions; the same five questions he answered yesterday, a week ago, a month ago, and the same questions he'll be asked tomorrow, a week from now, a month from now. It goes something like this:

RADIO PERSONALITY: "How 'bout your latest single?"

ARTIST: "Aww, it's doin' great . . . we just wanna thank the fans for takin' it to number one, and we just wanna thank folks like you for playing it."

RADIO PERSONALITY: "How 'bout your latest album?"

ARTIST: "Aww, we're real happy with it . . . this is the album I always wanted to do. And we wanna thank the fans for buying it."

RADIO PERSONALITY: "Hey, whaddya think of these fans out here today?"

ARTIST: "Aww, man, we just wanna say God bless the fans . . . they're the reason we're out here doin' this. We just wanna thank'em."

And so on. This interview is repeated in relatively unaltered form throughout the tour.

Anytime you're interviewing someone who is interviewed regularly, you face the challenge of coming up with new angles. Questions for which a pat answer won't do. That's where preparation comes into play. Work hard to come up with questions that haven't been lobbed at the person time and time again. Force your interviewees to examine what they are saying, what they have said, offer them the opportunity to explore new areas, and watch them light up and turn loquacious when you give them the chance to talk about something upon which they truly place some personal joy or value.

This point impressed most deeply on me when I was doing research for a piece on the drivers who pilot the giant buses that cart country stars from gig to gig. Radio is country music's bread and butter, so I was usually at the end of the interview line. I'd watch the artists do virtually the same interview over and over, watch their fixed smiles as they repeated all the catch phrases, thanked the fans, thanked radio, etc. Then I'd arrive, briefly explain my story, and say, "Tell me about your bus driver." It was a joy to watch their faces light up as they'd launch into a series of colorful anecdotes about bus drivers they'd known over the years. In a number of cases, I'd be invited on the bus to meet the driver and discuss the topic further. I still remember a gracious Vince Gill, long after closing as the final act in a four-day festival, taking time out to stand in the darkness outside his bus and tell tales on his driver. Like so many of the artists I interviewed, he welcomed the chance to cover some new ground.

The angles are always there. You just have to work a little harder than the next person to find them, but the payoff is worth it. You'll get quotes no one else will get.

## The *60 Minutes* Interview

I'm no Mike Wallace, and I know it. The most controversial reporting I've been involved in to date involved a pair of water towers, each shaped like a giant peach. While doing some preliminary research for an article on water towers in general, I discovered that not only did Town B (with permission, as it turned out) copy Town A's prize peach tower, Town B lifted a photograph of Town A's "Peachoid" and used it on its Web site, with Town B's name pasted roughly over Town A's name.

Well, you can imagine the ensuing scandal. But I hung in there. I asked the tough questions, got the answers. I suspect that if you were to look up Town B's Web site these days, you'd find the proper peach in place.

But I'm still no Mike Wallace. So when it comes to difficult interviews, I'd be talking out of school if I gave you too much advice. I do know that if the potential for controversy exists, the research phase of your interview is of critical importance.

There are any number of reasons an interview may be difficult to obtain, and not all of them involve the cover-up of state secrets. Perhaps the individual isn't interested in any exposure. Perhaps the individual has been overexposed. Perhaps the individual mistrusts the publication you're representing. Perhaps the individual just doesn't want to talk to anybody.

If you're faced with the big "no comment," remain cordially persistent. If you feel the individual is simply trying to duck a controversial issue, you may get a foothold by explaining that you are interested in doing a balanced piece in which his or her view is represented.

You might also do what you can to ensure that your requests are being accurately relayed. I've had interview requests sputter until during a follow-up call I discovered that someone in the chain of [mis]communication had confused my request.

In the end, it all comes down to clout and leverage. You either have it, or you don't, and if controversy is afoot, nothing else will be of use in getting sources to talk.

## The Simple Phoner

In my formative freelance days, I wrote brief features for a regional business newsletter. The editor was familiar with the business community, and often provided me with a list of contacts and phone numbers when he assigned a story. I'd sit down at the keyboard and prepare a set of questions. Then I'd start at the top of the list and make my calls. Once I reached the person I was after, I introduced myself, told him or her what the topic of the piece was, and asked if the person was willing to go on the record. If the person replied in the affirmative and said they had the time, I'd conduct the interview then and there.

I still do a number of interviews this way. If possible, clump your interviews together. It takes a while to get into "interview mode," and once you're in it, it's easier to maintain it than restart it another day. Interview clumping makes topical sense, as well. While working my way through a list of contacts for the previously mentioned piece on water towers, I began to notice a few recurring themes I might have missed had the interviews been conducted days apart. And because I was interviewing several different people on a similar subject sequentially, I was able to incorporate questions about those themes "on the fly," rather than making a callback six days later, when the topic had cooled and the interviewee had moved on to other things.

Here are a few more tips about phoners:

**Don't Call Us. . . .** If your subject has agreed to a scheduled phone interview, try to arrange that you call them. This helps you avoid a situation in which the person you're to interview calls twenty minutes early, catching you unprepared or even catching you gone. When you make the call, you have the opportunity to gather all your resources and switch over to interview mode.

**Phone versus Face.** If you can get all the information you need by making a twenty-minute phone call, why spend time traveling to a face-to-face meeting? If all you need is straightforward information for a straightforward informational piece, the phone should serve you well. And if the only option you are given is a phone interview, well then, that's your only option. On the other hand, keep in mind that a face-to-face interview yields observations, insights, and opportunities a phone interview never will. A phone interview with Aaron Tippin would have cost me a scene in which we stood face-to-face when I mentioned that I had once panned him in a review for what I thought was a cheesy prop. He was less than two feet away, muscle-bound, and wearing a camouflage cap. He looked me right in the eye and explained his position on the issue in question. It was an uncomfortable moment, but it lent the piece tension and made good reading.

**Don't Make 'Em Wait.** If you have call waiting, disable it. Don't get caught saying, "I'm sorry, Mr. President, I just need to take that call."

## The Conversation

An interview is best if it proceeds like a conversation, but the conversation must have structure. As in any conversation, you'll likely start off with a few pleasantries, a little "getting to know you." This is essential, especially if there is to be some depth to the interview, but don't waste too much precious interview time on meteorological banter.

As I mentioned earlier, I come prepared with a list of questions, but I don't spend much time looking at it. Try to maintain as much eye contact as possible. A quick glance at your question sheet now and again will suffice. And don't make a big production out of ticking off your listed questions as you ask them. This can be very distracting for the person being interviewed. If you proceed straight down your list and make a sweeping slash through each question as it is asked, your subject will end up trying to count questions, thinking, "Only two more to go." I generally ask the question, wait until the person begins answering, and then make a small check in the margin just to the left of the question.

Our best conversations usually occur with someone with whom we share an interest; with someone whose company we truly enjoy. During the conversation, you listen carefully, paying close attention. When the person looks at you, they see a true, active interest in your eyes. If you can duplicate this type of exchange during your interview, you'll elevate it from a process in which you are extracting information to a process in which the subject is freely sharing. Despite the fact that I used the word "duplicate," I don't mean to infer that you'll have to contrive this conversational "feel." Most of the people I interview *are* very interesting, or have something very interesting to say. When you stop thinking of an interview as a distinct process and begin to treat it as a more informal, loosely constructed exchange, the material you mine will be much richer. Listen actively—don't be so focused on the next question that you miss an important opportunity to digress. These digressions from the "script" are frequently fruitful.

Don't forget to listen for what the person *isn't* saying. They may be offering you an opening. Take it.

And of course, a little flattery rarely hurts. This isn't as obsequious as it sounds. Flattery doesn't have to be overt. We've all seen interviews in which the interviewer drooled all over the person being interviewed, and that's just plain ugly. It humiliates both parties. The very best form of flattery is familiarity, and that speaks directly to our earlier discussion on preparation. If you do your homework, it's likely that the person you're interviewing will be able to tell; and unless your homework uncovered actionable indiscretions on that person's part (indiscretions that throw you into Mike Wallace mode), you're likely to be rewarded with good material.

## Look Who's Talking

Having just explained my philosophy of interview by conversation, let me reinforce that an interview is not about you. You want your subject to do the talking. Don't waste precious interview time rattling on about yourself. Don't interrupt. Don't jump in with unnecessary corroborations of what your interview subject just said (one of my major weaknesses). Your input should be limited to comments and questions that keep the interview moving. I've gotten better at this over the years, but I still talk too much. The best way to cure yourself, based on my experience, is simply to play back the taped interview. I have yet to record an interview in which my extemporaneous blathering stood in favorable contrast to the words of the person I interviewed.

Humiliation and embarrassment are fine teachers.

## Be Prepared to Take What You Can Get

Not all interviews transpire at your leisure. I've learned to take what I can get, when I can get it. Assigned on short notice to get an interview with country duo Brooks & Dunn, I was told by their road manager that the pair was booked solid for the day with radio and television interviews. I was working on a story with a fairly narrow focus, and so only needed to ask two or three questions. Invoking polite persistence, I told the road manager this. Still no dice. "I tell you what," I said, noting that the performers' bus was parked about fifty yards from the backstage steps, "I'd be willing to interview them during the walk from the bus to the stage." The manager grinned, and told me what time to be back at the bus. When that time rolled around, I was there, tape recorder and notebook at the ready. When Kix Brooks stepped off the bus, his band was already onstage. I introduced myself, hit the "record" button, and started walking. Brooks was interested and attentive. His quotes were fresh and perfectly suited to the piece. We stood at the foot of the stairs as he answered my last question. On the interview tape, in the background, an announcer is saying, "Ladies and Gentlemen, *Brooks & Dunn!*" The crowd roared, Kix Brooks shook my hand, ran up the steps, and was gone.

When I did a story on a traveling butcher, I knew it would be a waste of time to sit down and do a run-of-the-mill interview. Instead, I got up at 5 A.M. and spent the day roaring around the country in his truck, stopping to stand in howling subzero winds as he butchered pigs barehanded. As soon as we'd climb back in the truck, the "interview" would resume.

## Earn What You Can Get

Access is often earned through trust. When I covered the same country music festival several years running, the promoter provided me with better and better access each ensuing year. Why? Well, for one thing, he's a promoter, and he understood that my writing translated to publicity. But he'd also been watching me. He knew I wouldn't take advantage of my access to be what performers refer to as a "germ" (hard "g"); that is, someone who leverages his or her sliver of access to "hang" with stars or hunt autographs.

Not only did this trust pay off in terms of general access, it paid off in situations in which I had to "wing" an interview. More than once the promoter intervened on my behalf with a road manager, vouching for my reliability.

You never know who's watching. Sent out (on short notice again, a hallmark of "live" country music journalism) to get an interview with performer Martina McBride, I was told by one of her "people" she would be doing only previously scheduled radio interviews and a "meet and greet" with her fan club. Fair enough, since I had had no previous contact with her management. I went about my business, interviewing several other performers, some on the fly, all expeditiously. One of McBride's management crew had been in and out of the media tent, and when I approached him for one last try in the "polite but persistent" mode, he agreed—based on his watching my work with other performers—to let me interview the singer on her way from the media tent to the "meet and greet." I did, got what I needed, and found McBride was engaging and gracious.

Which brings me to another point about persistence: "Getting to" prominent people can become a tricky dance you learn only if you're willing to risk getting your toes stomped now and again. But in more cases than not, it has been my experience and the experience of many of my colleagues that once you make it through the layers of insulation, the "main attraction" is the easiest person in the chain to deal with. It's the person I call "the third cousin to the main attraction" who makes your day miserable.

A final note about earning access. Hard work and reliability will translate into more work. I'm no insider, but the editors who sent me to cover country music events knew I had a good track record for getting the goods without trashing their magazine's reputation in the process, and thus they were quick to feed me assignments. This makes me happy and prevents my starving.

## GAINING CREATIVE ACCESS

I recommend that you never attempt to obtain an interview without the blessing and backing of an editor. Having said that, there will be times when the term "freelancing" takes on expanded meaning.

I believe I can honestly say I've never lied to get an interview. I have told the truth creatively. I've made my way through security checks for which I was not cleared. I'm shy by nature, but calmly persistent and occasionally insistent. I've learned the virtues of patience, readiness, and opportunism.

Just remember—if you're about the business of gaining "creative access," you have no recourse when "busted."

And finally, never gain access by invoking the name of a magazine you're not working for. On two occasions, I have found myself with an opportunity to get "inside" a story if I moved immediately. On both occasions, I made a judgment call, said I was a freelance writer who wrote for Magazine X (the truth, although I didn't mention I wasn't on assignment at the moment). In both instances, the minute I had access I called the magazine and let the editor know what I was up to. I cannot state strongly enough that this was an editor I had worked closely with for a long time; I was confident that the story was something she would want me to act on.

In contrast to my acting based on an established relationship, I'm familiar with instances in which a writer used a prior association with a magazine to get special access to events and personalities. These things get back to editors, and you'll never work for them again. I've seen it happen.

### Respecting Limits

Whenever I agree to a time limit on my interviews, I make it a point to keep close track of the time. When I hit the limit, I offer to wrap things up, and I mean it. The payoff? The person being interviewed appreciates the professionalism, and nine times out of ten, offers to extend the interview. From the chief of the Belize National Fire Service to a United States congressman, from monster truck drivers to neurosurgeons, this technique has frequently earned me interview overtime.

## RECORDING THE INTERVIEW

I've encountered a surprising amount of debate in nonfiction circles regarding the use of tape recorders in interviews. John Hildebrand, author of the well-received *Mapping the Farm* and *Reading the River,* as well as a number of other nonfiction works, feels that a tape recorder is artificial and distracting in much the same way as a television camera. I very much respect Hildebrand and have learned much from him, but we disagree on this issue. In my experience, the note pad is far more distracting.

Initially, many people do seem self-conscious when I produce and turn on a recorder. But soon, and very soon if the interview is going well and the "conversational" mode—complete with eye contact—is achieved, the tape recorder seems all but forgotten. On the other hand, I find that an interview subject is far more likely to be put off stride by my breaking eye contact in order to make a written note. You can almost hear the person thinking "What did I say that was important enough to write down? Was it good? Was it bad? Should I rephrase? Recant?" John M. Wilson advises,

> Don't suddenly start scribbling madly when sources launch into revealing conversation; that's the quickest way to get them to clam up . . . use shorthand or develop your own system, so that you can jot down notes almost casually, without distracting the subject.

I don't know shorthand; my system is the "no look." I write my notes without looking at the paper. Through peripheral vision, I can see enough of the writing on the paper to avoid scribbling over previous notes.

I've read pieces that infer that legendary creative nonfiction writer John McPhee never uses a tape recorder. I've heard him say otherwise, in person. He does use a recorder very sparingly, preferring to take written notes, but pulls out a recorder when his subject is voluble, such as the captain in McPhee's *Looking for a Ship.* McPhee also turns to a recorder if he finds himself trying to cover an animated conversation between a group of individuals, especially if they are speaking a technical language. I believe he cited as an example a group of geologists arguing about the nature of a rock formation.

More thoughts on recording interviews:

• Heed John McPhee and don't let a tape recorder "lull you to inattention." I always take notes as if my tape won't turn out; that policy has saved my story more than once. But McPhee wasn't addressing mechanical failure; he was speaking more in terms of the spirit of the interview. Don't just sit back and let your tape recorder pay attention for you. Remain actively involved. The recorder records the interview, it doesn't drive the interview.

• A recorded interview can be invaluable if your story is challenged. A friend once quoted a physician making a controversial statement. The physician phoned in a rage, accused my friend of libel, and vowed to loose the hounds of justice. My friend responded by politely saying, "If you like, I can send you a copy of the transcript of the interview. If that's not good enough, I can send you a copy of the tape itself." At that point, she relented, and the issue was resolved.

• Position your recorder so that it is stable. I once did an interview and didn't notice that with every gesture the person I was interviewing made, the recorder was rocking back and forth. The entire recorded exchange sounded as though it was set to some sort of sampled drum-beat: "Tacketa-tacketa-tacketa." Like to drove me nuts, transcribing that beast.

• Know the range of your recorder. Not only do you want to be sure you're picking up your subject's voice, you need to keep in mind that you'll be picking up background noise. I've got a beat-up old Sony handheld recorder that has surprising pickup abilities; if I'm not careful, I sometimes pick up far more background noises and conversation than I want.

• If I'm interviewing on the move or while standing, I hold the running recorder atop my legal pad with my left thumb. This keeps the recording microphone pointed in the general direction of the interviewee, and keeps my right hand free for note taking.

• Before you leave the house, check the batteries in your recorder. And never sally forth without a backup set. Position the recorder so you can see the spindles spinning, and sneak peeks at them throughout the interview.

• Do you have a pause button or switch on that recorder? Don't punch "record" without checking "pause." Let me assure you from experience that discovering you've just recorded an entire interview on one millimeter of tape leaves you with a profound sense of disappointment. All the more reason to watch your spinning spindles.

Obviously, tape recording isn't always feasible. When I spent a day roaring up and down the Mississippi in an open fishing boat with an outdoor television personality, I knew better than to record the sound of wind, and relied on my pen and legal pad. When writer Darcy Frey shadowed Coney Island high schoolers daily for several months while gathering material for *The Last Shot,* his book about inner-city basketball, he eschewed a tape recorder for the obvious reason: he'd still be transcribing tape.

For short phone interviews, I generally sit at my keyboard and type my notes on the fly. For an extended phone interview, I use the record function on my answering machine—*but only after receiving permission and making it very clear to the person I am interviewing that the conversation is being recorded.* In many states, it's the law.

In the end, whenever possible, I believe the best system of documenting an interview lies in a combination of written and tape-recorded notes. Unless you possess world-class proficiency in shorthand, a tape recorder will capture dialogue with a degree of detail you'll never achieve simply by taking notes. And by supplementing your tape recording with written notes, you'll have a backup system that also includes observations you'll not pick up with an audio recorder.

## Postal Interviews

Amidst all this talk of tape recording and note taking and telephoning and interviewing on the run, I'd like to point out one other option:

an interview by mail. Earlier in the book I mentioned an essay in which I quoted a famous landscape architect. The information I required from this individual was very specific, and I wasn't working under a deadline, so I submitted my question via the mail. His reply was articulate and concise, and fit into the essay seamlessly. I've done the same thing via e-mail.

## FUDGE, ANYONE?

This sidebar will prove that I am truly committed to giving you the real-world goods. If I weren't, pride and shame would prevent me from sharing what I call "the verification follow-up fudge technique." My sense of humiliation is mitigated by the fact that I was taught this technique by a colleague whose work over the years has been sterling, and that I have only had to use it once.

I once secured a rare and difficult-to-obtain interview with an individual I'd be nuts to identify. The twenty-minute recorded phone interview moved seamlessly from topic to topic, and was fruitful beyond my fondest hopes. In a sequence of events that followed shortly thereafter and cannot be explained within the limits of professional competence, before I transcribed the tape I accidentally recorded over the interview. The only thing working in my favor was a set of backup notes I had taken. When I realized what I'd done to the tape, I sat down with those notes and a sense of deep-seated terror and went over and over them, wracking my brain and writing down every sliver of information I could recall about the interview. Then, when it came time to plug the holes, I obtained a brief "follow-up" interview, "just to verify a few comments Mr. ______ made." This interview consisted of me framing questions the like of, "Let me be sure I'm being clear on your position regarding Issue X. Would it be accurate to say you feel such and such and so and so regarding that issue?"

At which point, of course, the individual reiterated his position, plugging all the holes that needed plugging.

Except the one in my fool head.

### Sneaky Note-Taking

Have to ask a tough question of a tough cookie? A writer who spent his early years interviewing attorneys once shared this technique with me:

> "If the individual was on his guard, I'd ask the tough question right away. But as he answered, I'd maintain eye contact and be careful not to spook him by taking notes. I'd just nod, and not write down a thing.
>
> "Once he'd given his answer, I'd follow with a softball, the likes of, 'Now you attended law school where?' And then, while he rattled off his curriculum vitae, I'd studiously scribble away, jotting down everything he said . . . in response to my first question."

## GO BEYOND WORDS

The observations you make leading up to and during the interview are critical. When I arrived early for an interview at Aaron Tippin's remote Tennessee farm, I stepped out of the oppressive heat into the cool air of an old workshop. It was the type of shop you'd expect to find in any farm, filled with old parts, fishing poles, scattered tools, unfinished projects. High on a hook on one wall, I spotted an old green hard hat. A set of orange letters spelled out "TIP" on one side of the hat. Later, well into the interview, I asked Tippin about the hard hat, and the question turned out to be the launching pad for an exchange that became pivotal in the published piece in which Tippin defended his "common man" image. All the preparation and research in the world wouldn't have uncovered that hard hat; I'm just glad I noticed it and then brought it into our discussion. You never know where a chance observation will take you.

During the interview, take note (literally, but take care that it not become a distraction) of the environment, of the subject's dress, appearance, mannerisms, demeanor. Is something else going on in the background? What noises can you hear besides your own voices? What color are the walls? Is the individual sitting or standing?

And so on. It is my firm belief that nothing is worth omitting. Chances are, you'll only use a thing or two from these notes in your article, but the observations serve a further purpose. When you're reviewing the transcription of the interview, they serve an evocative purpose; they add an entire dimension to the words. Even if you don't mention in the text of your piece that Elvis was seated on a pumpkin during your discussion of the postmodern grunge movement, the notation will trigger a more detailed recollection of the experience, and such recollection is critical when you want to move beyond simple transcript recitation.

## FINDING DIRECTION THROUGH TRANSCRIPTION

The process of transcribing a taped interview is boring, laborious, and time consuming. But beyond the obvious functional necessity of converting sound to type, the process of reviewing a taped interview provides you with a fresh opportunity to gain insight on your story and your subject. Back in your office, the subject's words often suggest a structure to the story that you may not have anticipated. In some cases, based on something your subject said, you'll discover an entirely new direction or theme for the story. Many a good quote translates to an excellent intro or conclusion. Background noises often trigger your powers of recall when it comes to recreating the scene of the interview.

## AS ALWAYS, GIVE THANKS

I always try to send a note of thanks to anyone who has helped me along the way to an interview. From the subject of the interview to that person's handlers, a thank-you has a way of easing your access should a return engagement be required.

# CHAPTER ELEVEN

# WRITING THE ARTICLE

Well, writing the article is the crux of the whole thing, isn't it?
Perhaps I should begin by telling you what this chapter *isn't:*

- It isn't a template. There is no "typical" article.
- It isn't a writing course, although an extensive section on writing is included.

This chapter *is* a guide to the *process* of writing an article, whether it be 50 or 5,000 words in length. I'll touch on the stylistic and theoretical, but in general I'll try to keep things fairly concrete and functional.

## CHOOSING A TITLE

Does choosing a title seem like a good place to start? It's not. When it comes to choosing a title for your piece, let me spare you a wad of wasted time and effort by sharing two words of advice: Don't bother.

Near as I can tell, nothing tickles an editor like coming up with a winky little title. Puns reign (there's one now). A profile of FBI director Louis Freeh in *George:* "The Freeh World." A profile of San Francisco 49ers quarterback Steve Young in *GQ:* "The Arm with the Golden Man." An article on landfills in *Swing:* "Don't Dump on Me."

I can't keep up, and I don't try. When an article is finished, I bold-type something across the top intended to let the editor know what follows, but I don't spend more than a moment doing so. When I finished my article on big things, I sent it to *The World & I* simply titled,

"Big Things." It ran in print as "Larger than Life." When I finished my article on Wisconsinites' penchant for winter weight gain, I sent it to *Wisconsin West* simply titled, "Wisconsin Winter Weight Gain Article." It appeared in print as "Life in the Fat Lane." When I finished my essay about houses on hills, I sent it to *Orion* simply titled, "Houses on Hills." It appeared in print as . . . "Houses on Hills."

No one was more surprised than I.

I'm having fun with this, but the point remains: You won't sell your piece based on its title, and nine times out of ten or thereabouts, your title will be discarded anyway, so when you finish your piece, tag it with something simple, stick it in the mail, and move on. When your comp copies arrive in the mail a few months later, you can find out what they named your baby.

Having completely dismissed the concept of titling, let me give a dissenting view equal time. In *Magazine Writing That Sells,* author Don McKinney speaks from his experience as an editor:

> [A title] not only makes clear what you're trying to say about that subject, but it helps you focus your material as well. Nine times out of ten, when an article came in with a title like "Clint Eastwood Story," the piece itself would reflect the same unfocused approach . . . a sharply written and carefully thought-out title will show the editor that you have a focus, that you know what your piece says. It's just another way to make a good first impression.

## WORD COUNTS

Word counts are used by editors to control the length of, and thus the amount of space consumed by, an article. If you are assigned a piece, you will also be assigned a word count. If you're writing a piece as an unsolicited submission, check the writer's guidelines of the publication to which you intend to submit the piece *before* you start writing. What word lengths do they accept? Is your article a feature, or is it intended for a specific section of the magazine? Does that section accept only short pieces? How short? Don't start writing until you know.

Word counts aren't hints. If an editor requests 1,000 words, she doesn't want 900 or 1,100. If a basketball coach asks you to go out and score 20 points for the team, and you score 40, you'll be the MVP. If an editor asks you for 2,000 words and you submit 4,000, the *editor* will be MVP: Mightily Vexed and Peeved.

It all comes down to allocation of space. In some cases, you'll be asked to trim a few words simply to make an article fit the layout. There are two ways to respond to this: A) righteous artistic indignation and refusal, or B) find a way to do it. Plan B tends to keep the work coming in, and is rarely an artistic compromise; as a matter of fact, you'll probably end up trimming something that helps tighten up the piece.

## THE OPENING OR LEAD

John McPhee advises writers to "write a lead that shines down into the subject like a light." Nice, eh? Of course, the tricky bit comes when you try to put that advice into practice.

The first words of your article are critical. They serve as your first impression in print. If they fail to draw the reader in, it's game over. I have a terrible time writing lead paragraphs, and often spend way too much time early on trying to craft the perfect opening line. Move on. Often the material you develop in the body of the piece will inform or suggest the development of the lead.

There are a number of ways to lead off an article. Here are a few.

**The Attention-Grabbing Quote.** Here are the first three words of my profile of outdoor television personality Dave Carlson for *Wisconsin West* magazine: *"LOOK OUT, DAVE!"* Like to know what happened next? I was banking on it.

**Ask a Question.** I love this Max Frankel lead, taken from *The New York Times Magazine:* "Heard any good obits lately?" If you haven't, you can bet Max has, and is going to share a few.

**The Challenge.** For the article on winter weight gain mentioned earlier, I began with this sentence: "You look like you've put on some weight." In our society, those are some of the rudest words you can utter. I was betting the reader wouldn't walk away.

**Set the Stage.** "In early 1969 my father suffered a stroke that paralyzed his right side and left him a cripple who had difficulty speaking whole sentences." What happened next? Why is the writer telling us about this personal event from the late '60s in a 1995 issue of *DoubleTake*? Where are we headed? Setting the stage with a simple statement of historical fact, author George Packer stimulates our curiosity. We instinctively crave context, and must read on.

**Set the Stage. Now. With Facts.** Like this: "The Year: 2052. The Place: *New* New York, a tidy, authoritarian metropolis no 20th-century resident of the Big, Bad Apple would recognize. Pristine. Well-managed. Safe. Enter Mike Danger." This straightforward "list" introduction to a review by Lamar Graham not only sets the stage, it sets a tone, and suggests things are about to happen.

**Lend Curious Insight.** "The octopus is the cleanest animal in the ocean! The *cleanest!*" By leading off his article in *Men's Journal* by quoting an animated chef, Glen Waggoner lets us in on the beginnings of something we may not know, and in doing so, hints that there is more to come.

**The Epigraph.** Also known as the *precede* (pronounced "pray-seed," accent first syllable). For my article about the cultural significance of water towers, I led off with an epigraph by a man referring to flight navigation but opening the door to greater metaphorical possibilities:

> "Water towers tell us where we are."
>
> —*Dave Westrate, private pilot*

My opinion is worth what it costs, but as far as I'm concerned, the king of the epigraph is Lewis Lapham, editor of *Harper's* magazine. The precedes adorning his monthly "Notebook" dispatches are consistently illuminating and comprehensively apt.

A caveat: Lapham aside, epigraphs or precedes are often a crutch of the neophyte. Don't go running off to your computerized quote generator in search of an easy maxim just so you have something to slap between the title and the opening paragraph. Lewis Lapham's epigraphs are not evidently apt; they serve to explicate the prose only after the prose has explicated them.

**The Sports Afield.** I call it that because that's where I learned it. It's been a while since I've picked up a copy, but when I was a young'n, every hunting or fishing article began with a wonderful pursuit. And then, just when something big was about to happen (a twig snapped, there was a tug on the line), the action stopped and the instructive exposition began. But then, after you waded through a treatise on scent application or the advantages of fluorescent rubber hula popper skirts, you'd reach the concluding paragraph, and the action would resume and resolve. The quarry was bagged, the fish netted, and it was off to the next adventure.

A warning about the *Sports Afield* style of introduction: I was recently involved in a discussion on this very topic with a fellow outdoorsman and writer. We were both reminiscing about wonderful childhood afternoons spent reading *Sports Afield* stories. We joked about the classic "take'em to the edge" intro. Then we both admitted something that revealed a fatal flaw in the technique. We both used to skip straight from the introduction to the conclusion!

**Cut to the Chase.** Sometimes you're better off to dive right in. Remember, the purpose of your lead is to hook the readers, get them to come along for the ride. Rather than dream up cutesy convolutions, sometimes it's best to come roaring right out of nowhere, so that by the time they've read the first three words, they're on the train.

You're more likely to go the "cut to the chase" route if you're writing short filler material, or something of a more academic nature. When I wrote a chapter on death by pulmonary embolism for a medical/legal text, I didn't spend a lot of time searching for the perfect embolismic anecdote.

## THE BODY

What you choose to put in the body of your piece depends on in which proportions you are serving art to content. The business of serving art is dictated by you and your muse, and the possibilities are endless. I've addressed a few of the possibilities in the large, general section titled "About Writing as a Craft" that follows.

For most of your freelance work, content will be dictated directly by an editor, and indirectly by the reader. Before you start writing, establish a clear understanding of your editor's expectations. In many cases, I talk to the editor about the "angle" he or she is interested in; I ask if there is anything I should know about the publication's readers that would affect my approach; I ask about preferences of style. Am I expected to *write* or *report*? Many of these things are covered in writer's guidelines, but I recommend confirming them with an editor, as policies change, and many editors are flexible.

Think about the magazine you're writing for. How much "artistic latitude" does it grant? Is its style light and conversational, or ponderous and literary? Is humor appropriate? Do any of the authors in the magazine's pieces (you *did* read a couple of copies of the magazine, didn't you?) use the first person? Is a question-and-answer format appropriate? Should you take an essayistic approach, or include lists and bulleted items? Are subheads appropriate?

Then think about the readers. I often try to write as if the readers were looking at my screen. Is my style appropriate? Do they get my jokes? Will they relate to my figures of speech? My slang? Am I being too dry? Would they prefer a different voice? Should I adjust the tone of the piece? Does my viewpoint serve the readers best? Would *I* sit through this thing and read it to the end? How does my article fit in with the rest of the content?

I also think about the reader trying to follow me. Does my progression through the piece make sense? Does the movement seem logical? Is it easy to follow, or are there points at which a reader might get lost? Are my transitions natural? Are there turns to miss? Have I made things more complex, difficult, or obscure than need be? Am I overly simplistic and predictable?

There are as many ways to approach a piece as there are writers and topics. When it comes to narrative structure, the nonfiction narrative can be as plotted as a novel. Writer Darcy Frey says that he attempts to establish a "through line"—that is, to identify a natural route of narrative progression suggested by the content itself. "I also think of a 'through line' as often not just a narrative progression, i.e., chronology, or storyline, but often an argument, or a line of thinking," says Frey. "Sometimes I try to explicitly pose or suggest a question in the beginning of a piece that I hope (and sort of promise the reader) will be answered by the end." Tracy Kidder attempts to find something "emblematic" in the narrative. John McPhee is famous for his "accretion of information." His "through line" is anchored to painstakingly collected and arranged facts—although all this talk of structure can get carried away. I once listened to (and found completely plausible) a workshop participant who explained in great detail how one of McPhee's pieces on geology was carefully stratified in order to reflect the geologic formation in question. Later that afternoon, in a question-and-answer session, McPhee appeared amused by this observation and indicated that he eschewed "that sort of thing." Of course, this is a bit like Michael Jordan saying he eschews any particular shooting technique. Technique hasn't been eschewed, it has been subsumed.

Some writers use an outline to chart their course. I've tried, gosh darn it, I've tried. But I've got to say that for me, the process is instinctive. To me, outlines are kind of like the instructions for assembling a set of particle-board bookshelves. I have a nagging feeling that I'd be a better person if I'd take the time to read them, and that my life would proceed in a smoother, more orderly fashion, but in the end, I get the bookcase put together anyway, and I'm just too stubborn to change.

Here's what I substitute for outlining: Before I begin writing, I read through all my notes, my interview transcripts, my photocopied research—everything. And while I do that, I type another set of general notes. By the time I'm done, not only am I refamiliarized with the topic, my new notes have often "clumped" in distinct groups suggesting form. I go from there. The "clump" technique. That one'll go down in literary history. (Sounds like a method for cultivating homegrown yogurt starter.)

And then I write. Don't fiddle around trying to get it perfect. Allow yourself a horrid first draft. Most good writers do. Go ahead and overwrite. You can't *re*write until you *write*-write. But I'm getting ahead of myself. We'll talk more about writing in the writing section to follow.

## THE WRAP-UP

I have heard John McPhee state that he always knows the last line of a story before he writes the body of the story. That's why he's John McPhee and I'm not. This I do know: the conclusion of an article should serve an active purpose. It is with the ending that you part company with the reader; it is the ending that will flavor the reader's reflective interpretation of the piece as a whole. When I was in junior high school, I recall that our music teacher always brought our symphonic cacophonies to peaceful resolution with a graceful descending sweep of her baton; the motion followed a path in the shape of a dotless question mark. I often visualize this motion when I read a well-written wrap-up.

In some cases, the ending of a piece should indeed serve as a utilitarian wrap-up, a review and summary of the body; a "what have we learned" type of discussion. This doesn't have to be as didactic a maneuver as it might sound. Consider the ending of Jeanne Marie Laskas' essay "What's Lithuanian?" from her book, *The Balloon Lady and Other People I Know:*

> I'm a journalist. I'm a Lithuanian. I'm an American. And I don't know what to do, either. The camera was rolling, and I was speechless, caught in the absurdity of the moment, this summit, this circus, where nobody seemed to hear anybody, nobody knew where to stand, and the journalists interviewed the journalists.
>
> The Cold War has ended and everything is topsy-turvy. Perhaps the girl on the west steps of the capitol heard the only definitive message to come out of this critical moment in history: "We-don't-know."

In other cases, the ending should reinforce the overarching theme of a piece. I tried to do this when concluding a piece on the cultural significance of water towers in America:

> I circled the catwalk twice. Rob had already finished hanging the flag, and it was time to descend. Looking to the blue hills in the distance, I misstepped, and leaned instinctively into the dense bulk of the tank. It felt cool, deeply solid. I thought of all this water, 50,000 gallons, 47 or so gallons of which—based on my water bills to date—I would draw before the day was over. Water is life, and as far as this town is concerned, this is the source. This tank, with its unseen pulse, its cycles of filling and emptying, is our communal heart . . . and threaded through the ground beneath us, to all edges of the place we live, are the vessels, the arteries from which we tap our own little daily portion. Today, when I pass the tower and look to the catwalk, I think of what I saw from that place above the ground but beneath the sky, and understand: *You are here.*

Sometimes an ending is effective if it echoes the introduction, takes the reader back to where the story began. This ending is sometimes referred to as "The Circle." In the introduction of a story about a group of country music bus drivers who have organized a charitable event called "Christmas Is for Kids," I quoted a driver called the "Fat Man":

> "We pick up our kids and meet at the First Baptist Church," says the Fat Man. "The church puts on a meal and entertainment. Santa Claus is there. Then we come on up here with these buses in a convoy. And man, they give us the street."

When it came time to end the piece, it seemed natural to echo the opening:

> They came to Hendersonville again this year. Fifty-one buses. Three-hundred-and-two children. And the Fat Man was there. He'd driven 165,000 miles since his last Christmas Is for Kids. Enough mileage to circle the earth six times and most of a seventh; endless miles spent fighting inclement weather, artless motorists, clutch-shredding grades . . . the clock. But when he pulled that land yacht into line and rolled it sweet and easy up Highway 31, it was smooth sailing.
>
> Man, they gave 'em the street.

And sometimes, the conclusion should, to paraphrase the great French poet and literary essayist Paul Valery, referring to the short poem, put you right through the windshield, ending unexpectedly, resoundingly. Again, I submit the work of Jeanne Marie Laskas:

> We drive into the woods and emerge through a clearing. We are on the runway. She stops, waits, then hits the accelerator, hits it hard. She wants to show me just how smooth this runway is. She is going fast. It indeed is a smooth runway. She is going faster—this is certainly one velvety smooth runway. She is going faster and faster and faster, and it seems as though we might take off, like in *Chitty Chitty Bang Bang.* She seems to want to drive the car right into the sky. She floors it. She delights in it. She is proud of it. She is 82 years old, and she is still cutting the grass on this runway, grooming it low and smooth, even though no airplanes land here anymore.

There is no "right" way to end any piece, but there are a number of effective ways, a handful of wonderful ways, and one perfect way.

Happy hunting.

## ABOUT WRITING AS A CRAFT

I have said that this book is more about freelancing than it is about writing, and it must remain so. By its very nature, freelancing requires from you a certain dexterity of style; in some cases I feel I am aided more by a knack for mimicry than the talents of a writer. The comments that follow are intended to address the craft, but they are also intended to address the fundamentals. You will find them to be wide-ranging and disparate—as wide-ranging and disparate as the assignments you'll be asked to take on as a freelancer.

Here we go.

### Free Writing

When I speak to teachers, I encourage them to give their students the opportunity to write without rules. Without fear of metaphorical knuckle-rapping in the form of infractions circled, slashed, and denoted in the margin. Without the possibility of taking a wrong turn, missing the point, or running afoul of the dictates of usage. To let them pick up words and play with them like the colorful building blocks they are. And then, perhaps through this play they will come to understand the possibilities of words and the craft of arranging them in answer to a voice that rarely issues from between the stiff covers of a guide to good grammar. The same is true for you. If you want to remain in love with writing, you must sometimes treat it the way we sometimes treat love; engage in it recklessly, pursue it with abandon. John McPhee, famous for his controlled, air-tight prose, allows himself (as he has said) a "hideous" first draft. Darcy Frey, a writer who produces wonderfully structured and nuanced nonfiction pieces for *The New York Times Magazine,* endorses the same philosophy. I find that I often peck and peck away at the introduction to a piece until I'm hopelessly log-jammed. And then I recall the lesson I seem to have to learn again and again: dive in, write without filters, just *type*! Knock loose the block that's keying the mass and let the story tumble out big, oversized, and ugly. Save the editing for later. The same philosophy holds true even if you're writing copy for a 30-second radio spot.

A quick qualifier: Having just disrespected grammar books, I want you to know that I follow my "write free, little writer!" comments with a clarification. I am not dismissing the importance of basic usage skills. Punctuation and vocabulary are the seasonings of writing. They add nuance to the power of the written word. A deft bit of punctuation does the work of an arched eyebrow in the telling of a sly joke; a rhythmic arrangement of words can make any piece sing. But save the finesses of punctuation for the revision stage (see "The Rewrite" section later in this chapter).

## Careful with That Thesaurus

Write naturally, plainly, simply. Don't get caught up in adornment. If you find yourself pausing to reach for the thesaurus—especially in early drafts—you're probably going after a word you don't need and your audience doesn't want to hear. My thesaurus is a mouse-click away, and I use it. But I police myself pretty strictly. If a word is a bit obscure, I ask myself: Will it trip my readers up? Can its meaning be inferred by the surrounding text? Are its illuminative properties worth its weight in syllables? Hold yourself to the simple but crucial standard Bob Bly sets with the maxim, "Write to express, not to impress."

## Show, or Tell?

Basing your writing career on aphorisms is as wise as basing anything else you do on aphorisms. The show-don't-tell versus tell-don't-show debate is a perfect example. Of course, the truth is, there is a time and place for each. It depends on the market. It depends on the audience. It depends on the word length. I once did a celebrity interview for a magazine in which I was allowed only 1,000 words. After an extremely productive face-to-face session, I had nearly an hour's worth of quotes. Given the combination of these two facts, it certainly didn't make sense to burn up a lot of the 1,000-word allowance with my ramblings. I provided just enough show-and-tell to set the scene, and then let the subject take over the telling. When I was putting the piece together, I thought of the two takes on showing versus telling and applied them as I thought appropriate. And that's the key. You can have all the instruction, all the hints, all the slogans you want, but in the end, you have to make the call. To a large extent, these calls are discretionary, based on intuition and experience.

## The Rewrite

Always, there must be the shaving and shaping. The tamping down. The part of writing where you twist the words around and around like a Rubik's cube, push a word backward, forward, cut it out, put it back in, stare at it until it seems a foreign tongue. I describe this part of writing as carving concrete with a spoon. The process of rewriting is as essential as it is interminable. And while the first flush of the free write is heady stuff, it is a fleeting crush compared to the deep sense of attachment that results from creating the compact, seamless tapestry in the rewrite. The thrill of the free write is analogous to the moment a sculptor conceives a masterpiece. The satisfaction of the completed rewrite is analogous to the moment when the sculptor backs away to regard the masterpiece made whole.

Learn to distrust your first draft. Resist satisfaction. Spurn the natural puppy love most writers feel for the first draft of a fresh idea and subject it to unforgiving scrutiny. Cut, rearrange, slash, rearrange, trim. Back away and review the structure of the piece. Did you take a wrong turn? Is the progression from introduction to conclusion easily followed? Assume the perspective of your readers. Is there reason to read beyond the first sentence? Does the content drive the piece, is the read a read with momentum?

Consider these things, and act on them.

## Write Out Loud

Early in my writing days, I heard it suggested that reading one's writing aloud was a useful technique in the process of rewriting. This seemed strange to me, and I resisted. I have a penchant for learning things the hard way. Eventually, however, I gave it a try. Turns out, it's indispensable. I still don't read aloud every piece I'm working on, but when it comes to knocking the kinks out of a particularly troublesome passage, nothing is better. It's a great way to hear what is forced, what is missing, where the rhythm has gone awry. What the eye passes over, the tongue will stumble over.

## Let Time Be Your Editor

Time is an excellent editor. The freelance life, with its irregular deadlines (and the tendency of some writers to procrastinate), doesn't always allow you to take advantage of the editorial services of time, but whenever possible, set aside your work after a few rewrites. Return to it two days, two weeks, a month later—as much time as you can spare—and previously obscure weaknesses will leap out at you like toads on a tablecloth.

## Discovering Your "Voice"

Think of your favorite writers: Chances are, you can identify their work simply by reading it. A byline isn't necessary. That's because they have achieved a distinct "voice." In the book *Creative Nonfiction,* Philip Gerard has this to say about voice:

> Voice is what the reader hears in his mind's ear, the strong sense that the words of the story are coming from another living, human personality with a unique perspective on events.

Voice is what lends authority to your writing. Voice is what invests your writing with personality. Voice stakes out your perspective. Voice has the potential to expand writing beyond information to communication. Voice, when you nurture it over time, becomes your signature.

I find the search for voice drives me as a writer as much as anything else. I continually search out assignments that give me the greatest opportunity to exercise and develop voice. One of the reasons I so love the genre of creative nonfiction is the opportunity it provides the writer to employ and enjoy the freedom of voice.

Perhaps it is a reflection of the schizophrenic nature of freelancing, but for me, the secret isn't in finding one voice for all pieces, it's letting one voice find me for each piece. Achieving voice is more a passive process than it is an active process.

Reading also plays a critical part in discovering voice. If you're passionate about writing, you read obsessively. After you've read, you find yourself mimicking what you've read. Read one writer and you've copied her; read 100 writers and you've developed your voice. Consider the words of T. S. Eliot:

> The poet's mind is in fact a receptacle for seizing and storing up numberless feelings, phrases, images, which remain there until all the particles which can unite to form a new compound are present together.

Another mundane qualification is necessary here, however. As a freelancer, you will be forced on occasion to conform—even, dare I say, *suppress*—your voice to match your assignment. You can rail against the artistic compromise inherent in these contortions, or you can view it as a writing exercise of sorts and cash the check.

## You Need Frank and Al

I have two friends. Colleagues, certainly; but friends, mostly. I'll call them Frank and Al. Let's talk about Al first.

Al and I have worked on a flotilla of projects together—mostly television and radio commercials. Each of these projects is a joint effort; we bring our creative ideas to the table, kick them around, hold them up to the light. Eventually, we choose a concept and begin the convoluted evolutionary process of development. Ours is a rare and invaluable creative relationship in that we feel completely free to share every concept, every scrap of an idea we might have for a particular project. We hold nothing back, and aren't shy about critiquing each other's ideas or recognizing those of quality. We have come to trust each other to the extent that we waste no time circling the issues, and we don't need to dance around each other's egos—although we both have them. At times it's like a good marriage: we disagree, we get grumpy, but respect for each other keeps it from getting personal, and in the end, we complement each other, producing higher quality work in tandem than we ever would separately.

Then there's Frank. Frank is a poet, a writer, and an experienced editor. Over the years, we've developed a collegial friendship, and often exchange works in progress. When I'm working on a piece that's giving me trouble, or when I think I've finished a piece, I run it past Frank. He works cheap (one cafe mocha and he'll edit all night), and won't waste my time saying things like, "Oh, I really like the part where you said love is like a red, red rose. . . ." He'll give me an honest, unsparing opinion. He's read reams of my writing, and as a result, knows my weaknesses, knows when to point to a passage of text and fix me with that look that says, "Now c'mon, you know better than this. . . ." It's invaluable. Sometimes when I'm developing a piece, I work and rework the words so many times I find I am no longer able to draw back and see the piece as a whole. It loses its structure, becomes a one-dimensional tangle. I am no longer sure of the original conceit. I refer to this as "going snow-blind." I am particularly prone to snow blindness while working on leads and conclusions, and it is wonderful to be able to show the work to Frank, knowing he'll give it a wise read, and then tell me quite simply if it works or doesn't work. We all doubt ourselves at times, and a solid opinion is precious. I was heartened once to hear John McPhee describe his own experience with snow blindness. His solution? He sent the troublesome introduction off to an editor friend. "I wanted to see," said McPhee, "if it worked."

I am not a joiner. I have participated in some productive workshops, but I've never belonged to a writer's group. Many people find support there, but I remain skeptical and reclusive. Human nature works against many writing groups. People tend to be either too polite or largely disinterested in the work of others, viewing the roundtable setting as simply an exercise in commandeering an audience. After all, we are all most interested in promoting *our stuff,* and why wouldn't we be? I think what you really need—if you want to grow as a writer—is one or two individuals you can trust to tell you the truth. Someone who respects you but isn't interested in stroking your ego. Someone who can look at your work and tell you what can be done better. In my case, Frank and Al fill the bill.

I encourage you to find your own Frank and Al equivalents. I'd give you their numbers, but they've got their hands full redirecting me.

# CHAPTER TWELVE

# THE SEND-OFF

I began the first draft of this chapter, "When it comes time to mail your article. . . ." In today's freelance world, that statement is rapidly taking on the ring of the archaic. These days, I submit the majority of my articles via e-mail. I still send enough work out by mail that they recognize me over at the post office, however, so we won't abandon the concept of stamps just yet.

## BEST FOOTNOTE FORWARD

I've written hundreds of pieces for a legion of editors. To date, I have met exactly three of those editors face-to-face. All three represent regional publications located in the part of the country in which I live. Every other editor I have ever worked for knows me only by my manuscripts.

Think about that the next time you're preparing to send your words on their way. Your manuscript is your personal emissary. It represents you. I'm not talking in the artistic sense, your soul on the page, that sort of thing. I'm talking about the fact that it represents you like a suit for an interview, that sort of thing. Whether you're snail-mailing or e-mailing your manuscript, you shouldn't let it go until you've fussed over it like it was a five-year-old being sent to the first day of kindergarten.

Perhaps that image is a bit overwrought. After all, it's not ribbons and bows and spitcurls an editor is looking for. An editor is looking for good material. But the cold hard facts are, you need every edge you can get, and proper presentation of your work can give you that edge. Before I turn into some sort of frenetic win-at-all-costs motivational sales coach, let me assure you that the freelance "edge" is not necessarily achieved by making a scene. The way to attract and *sustain* an editor's attention is not through funky stationery and bizarre behavior. The way to attract and sustain an editor's attention is to make his or her job easy. How do you do that? Let me try this distillation: Submit excellent material and make it easy to read. It's about that simple.

This chapter addresses the "easy to read" part.

## BEFORE YOU LISTEN TO ME

In the sections to follow, I'll outline what I know about the submission process. The principles I address are generally the "industry standards." Use them to familiarize yourself with the process and avoid basic mistakes. But before you submit your work to any outlet, check the writer's guidelines (you do have a set, don't you?) for their submission instructions. In some cases, those instructions are very specific. In Chapter Seven, we discussed the guidelines provided by *The World & I*; in addition to listing the type of articles the magazine is interested in, they contain a number of specific instructions pertaining to manuscript submission—ranging from proper paper size and weight to proper footnote style to the proper use of acronyms. Pretty specific stuff . . . more specific than I can provide.

## MAKE SURE IT'S EASY TO READ

To make an editor's first cut—assuming, in the first place, that you have submitted material appropriate to the market—you'll need to submit a neat, professional package. Work that is hastily tossed off, crumpled, smudged, stained, or otherwise neglected or abused will make a negative first impression. Fairly or unfairly, the cosmetic appearance of your work counts for something: don't obscure professional content with unprofessional presentation. An editor may also assume work that is crumpled, smudged, and stained has already "made the rounds."

Once you've made that first cut, your work will get a quick once-over. This is where the "easy to read" part comes into play. As you've no doubt guessed, I'm not talking in terms of an editor's reading ability, or your overall writing ability. I'm referring to how your manuscript *scans*. It should read smoothly and cleanly from top to bottom. Anytime an editor encounters a bump in the road, you run the risk of losing that editor. Bumps take many forms: typographical errors, misnumbered pages, strange fonts, clumsy corrections, incorrect line spacing, and so on. Will an editor actually discard an otherwise well-written or timely piece because of a typo? You bet, if he runs into the typo (or any other "bump") before he gets to the meat of your piece.

Legend has it that American poet and critic John Ciardi was once asked if he read every poem submitted to the *Saturday Review,* of which he was poetry editor. The exchange went something like this: "Yes," he replied, "I start to read every poem." The interviewer scoffed. Surely Ciardi was stretching the truth. The *Saturday Review* received thousands of poems. Again, Ciardi said, "I start to read every poem." Then he said, "I read to the first 'clinker.' Then I discard the poem and move to the next." Now the interviewer had a different question. "But isn't that unfair? To discard an otherwise wonderful poem because of one misstep." Ciardi was unmoved. "If you're auditioning a violinist for an orchestra, and the violinist hits a wrong note, you don't need to hear a second note."

You're up against an army of other writers; the early stages of the selection process can hinge on the tiniest of impressions—an editor has to start somewhere. As we move through the following sections, remember: we're assuming an editor will read your manuscript, and we're determined to make that experience as smooth as possible.

## PRESENTING THE PACKAGE

Many of the principles we discussed in Chapter Eight about query letters apply to manuscript submission. Dispense with ornamentation and go for a clean, professional look. Specifically:

- Do not put your manuscript on letterhead.
- Print on only one side of each sheet of paper. It's a shame about the trees, but nothing gives an editor ocular seizures like reversed type shadows.
- Use 8½ by 11-inch white paper of at least 16 lb. bond. Several sources recommend you use paper with a twenty-five percent cotton

blend; I don't, and things are going fine. Do not use very thin papers and erasable bond papers; type on erasable bond will smear.

• Place your name, address, phone and fax numbers, and e-mail address in the upper left corner of the first page of your manuscript. This information can be single-spaced and need not be repeated on subsequent pages. Some sources recommend that you include your social security number, as publishers must file payment records with the government; I don't care to send that information out any more than need be, and based on my experience, the fate of your piece is unaffected by the presence or absence of a social security number. The information is easily supplied when a contract is signed.

• Place the approximate word count of the piece in the upper right-hand corner of the manuscript. *Writer's Market* also recommends that you include the rights you are offering for sale and a copyright notice. Feel free, but the bottom line is, most magazines stipulate the rights purchased in the contract you sign. Your powers of negotiation are virtually nil. This is not to say you must surrender. On the contrary, you must be very aware of the rights you are selling, get it in writing, and don't assume you *must* cave to the whim of the magazine. My point is simply that typing the rights you are "offering" on your manuscript is largely a moot point. As far as a copyright notice, it really isn't necessary. Your work is copyrighted by virtue of its existence. I don't include one. The bottom line? Postings of rights offered and copyright notices are often the marks of a beginner.

• Beginning with the second page, number the pages of your manuscript. Using the page numbering feature of my word processing software, I place the number in the upper-right-hand corner of each page, and precede the number with a "slugline" consisting of my last name and sometimes a word from the title or descriptive of the topic.

• Center the title roughly one third of the way down the first page. I capitalize the first letter in each appropriate word of the title; others underline the title or type it in all capitals.

• One double-space below the title, center "by [Your Name]."

• Double-space your manuscript. Again, it's a shame about the trees, but a double-spaced manuscript is easier to read, and the extra space between lines allows an editor to make notations as needed.

• As a general rule, margins should run about 1½ inches top, sides, and bottom. Standards vary from publication to publication.

• My word processing program is preset at twelve characters per inch, and I leave it there. Other sources recommend ten characters per inch.

• Use simple, easy-to-read type fonts. Good choices are standard "serif" fonts such as Times and Courier. I cannot stress strongly enough how amateurish the use of frilly fonts looks. I used to copyedit for a regional magazine and was baffled by the number of folks who thought the editor was actually going to wade through 2,000 words of computerized calligraphy. And while I'm at it (indulge me a touch of crankiness here), SPARE YOUR EDITOR AN ALL-CAPS ASSAULT. Put quite simply, this is frightening.

An important digression regarding fonts: Many smaller magazines are now "scanning" stories with optical character recognition (OCR) software. The "cleaner" the font you use, the more accurately the piece is scanned. The more accurately the piece is scanned, the less copyediting and proofreading effort it requires. Furthermore, if a magazine up against a deadline is looking for a last-minute piece (writers aren't the only ones who procrastinate), and an editor has to choose between a clean piece that will scan easily and one that will give the OCR program fits, the clean piece is in.

• Indent paragraphs five spaces.

• Using continuous-feed paper? Separate all pages and remove the perforated edges.

• Fasten manuscript pages with a paper clip; do not staple. Unless specifically directed to do so, do not place your manuscript in a binder.

• If you use a typewriter or dot matrix printer, make sure your ribbon is fresh. If you use a laser printer, make sure your toner is full. If your printer fades, so will an editor's attention.

• I've always taken advantage of my word processor's italics function. While researching this section of the book, I've found that most folks recommend that text to be set in italics be underlined rather than italicized. Now we've both learned something.

• My farmer father writes wonderful letters. Up until a few years ago, he pounded them out on an old Underwood manual typewriter. When he made a mistake, he advocated what he grinningly called the "smash-over" method. He'd backspace, center his thick index finger over the appropriate key, and bash away until the mistake had been obliterated. While this makes for a fun little story and paternal correspondence with character, it will not win you friends in editorial circles. I suggest you opt for the judicious application of correction fluid.

• I always signal the end of the article by center justifying the word "End" like this:

- END -

John M. Wilson recommends three hash marks, center justified, like this:

# # #

Choose your favorite. Just make it clear that the text has come to a close.

Remember: These are general guidelines. Check your target publication's writer's guidelines for specific instructions. Don't expect them to address the smashover method.

## The Pen Is Mightier . . . Well, Not Any More It Isn't

We've all heard the story—or its equivalent—of the manuscript scribbled on cardboard scraps and soup labels that became a national bestseller. The fact is, you should never submit anything in longhand. The odds of your neatly typewritten or computer-generated work getting a fair review are slim; the odds of your handwritten work getting a fair review anywhere it counts are nil. To further drive this point home, the previous sentence as I originally wrote it read "*essentially* nil." An editor friend who read over the galleys of this book drew an emphatic line through *essentially*.

## It's OK to Copy

Never submit your only, original copy of any manuscript. If the manuscript is stored in a computer, this is not an issue. If not, submit a photocopy, but make sure it is clean, sharp, and perfectly aligned. Carbon copies are unacceptable curiosities at this point.

**Sample Manuscript Page**

Michael Perry
Mailing Address
City, State, ZIP
Phone
Fax
E-Mail

Approx 1500 words

Aaron Tippin/Truck Piece
by Michael Perry

A ways east of Nashville, there's a holler full of trucks. Eleven of 'em, a rough, beat-up bunch, faced inward on a semicircle. At one end of that semicircle is an old wooden shop. You can read a lot about a man by his shop. This one is generally organized, but retains the comfortable clutter of use. A worn stand-up toolbox stands front and center; a screwdriver handle and a few wrenches protrude from gapped drawers. A torn-down transfer case rests alongside a homemade straddle pit. There's an old yellow fridge covered in stickers, a plumb ugly bench upholstered in Naugahyde, a tiny, tinny boom box tuned to a country station, and a pair of dusty fishing poles. And hung on a hook on one wall, along with a mess of other things, an old forest green hard hat. On the side, in scuffed orange letters, it says, "98 TIP."

"TIP" is Aaron Tippin, the man who first caught the attention of country music fans in

## THE COVER LETTER

We discussed cover letters previously in Chapter Eight. When you're submitting an assigned piece, your brief cover letter should include the title of the article, a brief summary, and mention of the fact that the piece was assigned. You can accomplish this in brief fashion: "Enclosed please find the article on monster trucks you approved on spec in April. 'Monster Trux' describes recent advances in monster truck technology." A cover letter should also mention any additional enclosures, such as photographs. Finally, your cover letter is not a sales piece. Think of it as a packing slip.

## PUTTING IT IN THE MAIL

Don't stuff your version of *War and Peace* in a no. 10 business size envelope. If your manuscript is more than four pages long, consider placing it in a 10 by 13-inch manila envelope. You might be looking at a little more postage here and there, but if I were an editor, I'd much prefer a smooth sheaf of paper to a typewritten origami wad.

Be neat. If possible use envelopes with your return address preprinted (in a style matching your letterhead) in the upper left-hand corner. The editor's address should be centered on the envelope, typed or printed on a mailing label. If I'm submitting a manuscript in a large manila envelope, I use printed labels for both my return address and the editor's address. Follow U.S. Postal Service guidelines, including the use of all caps and proper postal abbreviations (ask for a copy of the guidelines next time you're in the post office). If you must address envelopes by hand, use neat block letters, all caps, also in the style recommended by the U.S. Postal Service.

When I submit a manuscript that has been assigned or approved on spec, I make a neat notation in red ink above the editor's name: *Requested Material.* This prevents my piece being tossed in a slush pile somewhere. John M. Wilson recommends a notation in the lower left-hand corner of the envelope: *Enclosed Manuscript Assigned and Expected.* I like his idea better. Beyond those two specific references, don't festoon your envelope with doodles, cutesy stickers, or pleas for attention. Such gimmickry is unprofessional and unwelcome, and will be received and treated accordingly.

Always enclose a stamped, self-addressed envelope for unsolicited or spec submissions. If you want your manuscript returned, be sure the SASE is large enough to accommodate it, and that it is accompanied by sufficient postage (note: for submissions sent outside the United States, your SASE will need to be accompanied by International Reply Coupons rather than U.S. stamps; ask for details at your post office). Personally, I find it more expeditious to simply include an SASE with one first-class stamp. I note on my cover letter that the manuscript is stored on disk and need not be returned. Some writers skip the SASE and enclose a self-addressed, stamped post card with a checklist of editorial options ("accepted," "rejected," "accepted with changes," etc.) and space for editorial comment. If I'm sending material on assignment, I skip the SASE.

### The Envelope, Please

Here's an interesting tidbit shared with me by an experienced (but unfortunately not powerfully connected) editor: Because many beginning writers are loathe to even crease their precious work, they slip it with great care into a large 9 by 12-inch manila envelope. Seems like a good idea in theory, and I do warn against jamming *War and Peace* in a number 10 business envelope. But this editor pointed out that whenever his mail was brought to his desk, it was neatly stacked: Two piles of number 10 business envelopes, stacked side by side and *on top of* the larger manila envelopes. As the day progressed, he worked his way through the stack. By default, he got to the manila envelopes later in the day—when the odds of his being swayed by a nice, crease-free manuscript had long since faded.

Is that the kind of inside tip that will make or break your freelance career? No. But now you have something to bring up over coffee the next time you need to set a fellow writer to second-guessing.

## POSTAL OPTIONS

I mail virtually all of my work first class. Other options are less expensive, but first-class mail receives better handling and is delivered more quickly. First-class mail is also forwarded for one year and returned automatically if undeliverable—an advantage with practical implications in the "here today, gone tomorrow" world of publishing.

In some cases—when following up on an unresponsive editor, for instance—you might wish to use certified or registered mail. If you're in a deadline jam, consider priority mail or overnight services provided by companies like UPS or Federal Express.

Each year, *Writer's Market* provides updated postal information inside its front and back covers, but don't forget your most obvious source of information: the person behind the counter at your local post office. We all like to complain about the USPS, but I must say the folks at the two post offices I've done the majority of my dealings with have been very helpful when explaining my postal options, and chances are you'll find the same thing to be true.

Remember—if you're corresponding with a magazine outside the United States, your SASE with U.S. stamps won't work. You'll need to purchase and include International Reply Coupons (IRCs) instead. They aren't available at all post offices. Like the one in my town, for instance.

## Mailing Photographs and Slides

In Chapter Seven, we discussed how you can enhance your ability to get assignments by providing photographs and illustrations. If you submit prints, slides, or illustrations, always mail them first class. In some cases (especially when mailing slides or original artwork), you may wish to send them by certified or registered mail, so they can be tracked. You should probably also enclose sufficient postage for the return of your materials, although it has been my experience that when I submit photographs or illustrations, I am doing so on the request of an editor who will cover the postage for their return.

Photos and original artwork require extra protection in the mail. A piece of cardboard slipped into an envelope will help; better yet, inexpensive photo mailers are available at most office supply stores and some photography supply shops.

Photographs and illustrations should be labeled, captioned, or numbered as indicated by the guidelines of the publication in question. I never send out a photo or illustration without my return address and phone number attached to the back.

## ELECTRONIC SUBMISSIONS

As of this writing, none of the last six articles I wrote ever passed through the U.S. mail until they were delivered to readers as part of a magazine. Electronic submissions are becoming *de rigueur*. It makes sense: when I zap an article over the phone lines, it can be downloaded directly into a magazine's computer layout, obviating a number of time-consuming steps in the process.

In my case, "electronic submission" generally means an article sent directly from my personal computer to that of an editor, via e-mail. I simply copy the text from my word processing file, paste it in an e-mail message frame, and send it on its way. (You can simply e-mail the file itself, but I have encountered problems with garbled, unintelligible text at the editor's end with this method.) Be aware that text characteristics like italics or underlining may not transmit; it's a good idea to fax a copy of the piece for an editor's reference, and make sure you get a chance to review galleys of your work before publication.

Also included under the aegis of electronic submissions are faxes and computer disks.

### Submissions by Fax

Occasionally, you'll be asked to fax an article to an editor, and that's the only time you should do so. Unsolicited faxes are rude and unwelcome. It's generally a good idea to follow your fax with a call, to make sure it has made it—in its entirety—to the person for whom it was intended.

### Submissions on Disk

If you are asked to submit material on computer disk, first make sure you understand exactly what the publisher needs, from the size of disk to limitations on formatting. For instance, a publisher to which I regularly submit material on disk asks that certain commands, including those for creating bold or italicized text, not be used, as the underlying code disrupts the computer system they use for layout. This publisher provides me with very specific writer's guidelines for electronic submissions, as will most publications who solicit work in this form.

At the very least, I always include the following information on the disk label: The name of the file in which the manuscript is stored; the name and version of the word processing program I used; and my name, address, and phone number.

Last, I advise that you always use disk mailers. Disks are notoriously unreliable, and the better you can protect them in transit, the better your chances that the information they contain will be retrievable upon arrival.

### REMEMBER . . .

Remember the Alan Burdick quote in Chapter Seven and be sure you've addressed your material to the proper editor. Don't know who that is? Make a brief phone call to the publication and ask.

## TRACKING YOUR SUBMISSIONS

It's critical that you keep track of your submissions. I simply log them in a word processing file, noting title, word length, date sent, market (name of publication), and editor. I also note if the piece was accompanied by any enclosures (i.e., pictures, supplementary information, sidebars, etc.). Simultaneous submissions are grouped and marked as such. If the piece is rejected or accepted, I so note.

I also have a general notes section. I use this space to list potential markets and record editors' comments.

The CD-ROM version of the 1997 *Writer's Market* includes a program for tracking submissions.

## IT'S OUT THERE. NOW WHAT?

Most publications in *Writer's Market* list a reporting time, but these are sometimes arbitrary. Generally, if you submit an article on spec, or submit unsolicited material, you should allow a month for the editor to respond before sending a brief, polite follow-up note inquiring as to the status of the piece. If another three weeks pass, follow up with a brief, polite phone call. You'll learn through experience how to work within these parameters. As John M. Wilson says, "You'll have to learn to be as pushy or as patient as good judgment and individual situations suggest." It's true.

If your piece returns rejected read the section on rejection in Chapter Seven and shoot it right back out there.

### Check Your Spellchecker

When it comes to high-speed trolling for typos, there's nothing like a powerful computerized spellchecker. I sure do like mine, and use it often. But recognize its limitations. You wrote "your" where you should have written "you're"? Your spellchecker probably missed it. "There" for "their"? Same story. Always proof your work with the ol' eyeballs before you put a stamp on it.

## EDITORS

Who are these editors to whom we send our hopeful queries and polished prose? Who are these people with the power to publish or cause us to perish? Who are they, and how do we act in their presence?

Don't be intimidated. Editors aren't looking for adversaries, they're looking for someone who can deliver good work in a timely manner. You say you can do that? Well then, no worries.

Turns out, editors are a fairly normal bunch. Oh sure, a few are renegades, societal high-flyers, raving autocrats, or frosty intellectuals, but for every one of them, there are a legion of other editors who share an experience very similar to yours: They're simply trying to do a job, to do it well, and frequently to get it done under deadline.

Editors are *not* writing coaches, and they're not counselors or therapists. They don't have time to nurture your image of yourself as quirky *artiste* or indulge your weeper of a frustrated writer's life story. Having said that, the best editors are a rich repository of writing refinements. I have received some of the finest writing instruction of my life from editors who took the time to make suggestions regarding my copy. Not everyone is so receptive. When I worked as a freelance copyeditor for a magazine, I found it interesting that the writers who complained most loudly about adjustments to their work were usually those who needed it the most. The editor and I frequently fantasized that the finest revenge we could exact from these cranky types would be to publish their work exactly as submitted, for all the world to see and jeer. As a writer hungry for publication, I was always amazed at the opportunity these would-be writers were willing to squander in order to nurture their egos.

When you find an editor who likes your work, cultivate that relationship assiduously. Don't get chatty or pepper the editor with spur-of-the-moment ideas, but keep the *quality* proposals coming at a regular but respectful pace. Don't hound your editor, but do take proper advantage of the relationship, and at regular intervals ask if any assignments are available.

Yes, cultivate the relationship, but do not fall in love with an editor. You will get your heart broken. Why? Well, freelancing is tough, but editing is no stick of cotton candy either. New management cleans house, downsizing strikes, editors are fired, editors transfer, magazines die, heck, *editors* die. I once had a humor piece accepted by an editor with the proviso that I make a few rewrites. I did, and sent the piece back. A few months passed with no reply. Finally, I made a follow-up call, and I must admit there was just a hint of "snooty" in my tone. Of course, when I got the news that the editor had passed away, I expressed my condolences. And forthwith asked if the magazine was still interested in the piece. They were. A sale is a sale.

Of course, if you're in the business long enough, you will run into the occasional bad egg, and you'll have to make a decision: Do I put up with inconsistent, incompetent, or heavy-handed editing simply to get published? How many broken promises constitute the unforgivable lie? Is the bad karma worth the gig? As long as you can honestly tell yourself the problem lies with the editor and not your own territorial feelings about your writing, don't be afraid to move on. You may even be able to find someone else at the magazine through whom you can funnel your work for better results.

Above all, be honest with your editors. Remember, they work with writers every day. They understand procrastination. They've heard every ornate excuse under the sun (they're frequently conceived under the moon, by the way). If you're in trouble with a project, say so early. Maintain contact. Work with the editor toward a solution. A good editor knows the difference between someone struggling toward a solution and someone simply dropping the ball. Finding your way through these situations can be uncomfortable, but when handled professionally and properly, the experience will likely result in a stronger relationship.

# CHAPTER THIRTEEN

# SECONDARY SALES

Once you sell an article, don't let it get dusty. Move it on out again.

Reselling, or reslanting and *then* reselling, articles is something I would do well to concentrate on more frequently. I've made my share of secondary sales, but quite frankly, I tend to finish a story and move on. As a result, I'm missing opportunities to coax a little additional income from each piece.

Think of article resales this way: You did all that work on a story, why not let the story work for you?

## FIRST, ABOUT RIGHTS

Before you sell an article a second time, be absolutely sure you have the right to do so. Before I reprinted my essay, "Shooting the Split on the Way Home," in my book *Why They Killed Big Boy . . . & Other Stories,* I checked the contract I signed when the piece originally appeared in *The Christian Science Monitor.* It stipulates:

> *The Christian Science Monitor* retains the rights to an essay or poem for 90 days after publication. After 90 days, the rights return to the author. We do not accept previously published submissions.

Since a year had passed since the essay appeared in the *Monitor,* I knew I was free and clear to reprint it elsewhere. Rights vary (see sidebar, "Know Your Rights"); before you approach secondary markets, be sure you very clearly understand the nature of the rights you retain. Also be aware that simply changing the title and lead of a piece and calling it "new" isn't enough to keep you out of legal hot water if you're selling first rights, or trying to resell a piece to which you previously sold all rights.

The paragraph from the contract quoted above includes an additional bit of information pertinent to this chapter: Some markets will not accept material that has appeared elsewhere. Before you burn time, supplies, and postage sending out previously published material, check the target publication's writer's guidelines to see if they'll even consider it.

## SECONDARY SALES OVERVIEW

In some cases (keep our brief discussion of rights in mind), you'll be able to resell your original article, verbatim. In other cases, a change in tone or slant will be required. In still other cases, you'll be able to sell bits and pieces of the article as "filler." And of course, an incidental segment of one article may provide the central topic for a spin-off piece.

## SELLING THE SAME THING TWICE

Assuming you've retained the legal rights to do so, there's no better way to get a good return on your words than by selling something you wrote once, *more* than once. After my article on farm auctioneers appeared in *Wisconsin West,* I searched *Writer's Market* for a secondary market. When I saw that *Capper's* was looking for material "emphasizing home and family for readers who live in small towns and on farms," with "a Midwest slant," and that the publication "accepts previous submissions," I dropped a copy of the piece in the mail. *Capper's* purchased and reprinted an edited version. After a humorous piece on my blundering inabilities as a bowhunter was published by *International Bowhunter,* it found a subsequent home at *North American Whitetail.* After "Courtin' Country Style," a semicomic memoir of my semicomic teenage dating experiences, appeared in *Wisconsin West,* it traveled southward to Indiana's *Electric Consumer,* a regional publication for rural electric customers.

Apart from working within the legal constraints of rights sold, be completely up-front with editors when pitching a previously published piece. Want to make a lasting impression with an editor? Sell a piece to that editor and wait for her to discover (and the odds are better than you might believe that she will) she was serving seconds. In the cover letter accompanying a piece offered as a resale, I state when and where the piece appeared previously, and include information about the original publication, including its location, audience, and range of circulation. Sometimes you'll get a pleasant surprise. I figured the odds were pretty good that a regional publication from Indiana wouldn't mind reprinting something that had appeared in a publication covering western Wisconsin. But I *was* surprised when *North American Whitetail* took the bowhunting piece, as there seemed—to me, at least—to be some overlap. Apparently not, or at least not to the extent that it concerned the editor.

## MAXIMIZING YOUR PER-ASSIGNMENT EARNING POTENTIAL

With section headings like this section's, late-night infomercials have got nothing on me. So put down that remote and be prepared to be amazed as I share never-before-revealed (weeell . . .) secrets to double, triple, nay, *quadruple* your writerly income. Cue the disclaimer, pass the exclamation marks, and read on:

### Start Early

When you get an assignment for an article, consider how the topic might be expanded or refocused to fit other markets. Whenever possible, pitch and secure additional assignments in advance. Then, when you do your research and conduct your interviews, you can get information for several projects all in one fell swoop. When a regional newspaper hired me to cover a four-day country music festival a few years ago, I realized I'd have time and access to work on additional stories. And so I faxed a copy of the scheduled artists to an editor at *Country Weekly* with whom I'd worked previously, and followed up with a phone call to see if she was interested in any profiles. She wasn't, but she sent me to another editor who wanted a piece on festivals in general, and he gave me an assignment. I also took advantage of my presence at the festival to pitch and secure another assignment from a general interest magazine, profiling "life on the road" from the viewpoint of the artists' bus drivers. One assignment parlayed into three.

## Examine the Topic at Hand

Does it suggest its own "angles"? Does the piece focus on a person? Man or woman? If, for instance, you're writing a piece on trademark law for a business magazine, and one of the individuals you'll be interviewing is a successful female trademark attorney, think: Is there a potential article here for a women's business magazine? How about a mainstream women's magazine? Perhaps a profile for a legal journal? An update on trademark law for an inventor's magazine? And so on. (It might not hurt to reread the second half of the "Writing What You Think Will Sell" section of Chapter Six.)

Sometimes the potential for expanded markets won't hit you until you're well into the piece, or even until after the piece is complete. Whatever the chronology of the process, there are many ways to generate additional sales. A few thought-starters follow:

## Spin-Offs

I once wrote a brief piece for a regional business newsletter detailing the rise of medical transportation services. One of the business owners the editor asked me to interview was a woman. With no prior business experience, the mother of two children had started a "medical taxi" service and turned it into a successful small business. Nearly two years later, I sold an updated, expanded version of the original piece to a national women's magazine. By changing my focus from "medical transport" to "successful female entrepreneur," I had a new article.

## Expansions

Another time, I wrote another brief "overview" piece describing corporate libraries in the city where I lived. Using that piece as a starting point, I expanded it to include corporate libraries in general, refocused it to a writing (as opposed to business) audience, and sold it to *ByLine.* And if you've read this far, you'll have discovered by now that I further updated and reworked the piece to fit within the pages of this book.

## A Narrower Focus

Interviewing a prominent chemist for a general interest piece on recent developments in organic chemistry? Would the alumni publication from the chemist's alma mater be interested in a profile? How about his hometown newspaper? You say the chemist loves to rehabilitate old steam engines? Perhaps an article for *Live Steam* is in order. Now forget the chemist. How do these "recent developments" affect daily life? Where are they being put into use? Better-tasting decaffeinated coffee? Sounds like a filler for a coffee trade magazine. Paint that dries more quickly? An update for *Home Magazine* might earn an extra nickel. Just as it is critical to get the "big picture" when writing an article, it is critical to get the "little picture" when expanding the marketability of the information you gather.

## Unforeseen Topical Connections

Sometimes topical connections surprise you. Based on my experience as a cyclist and my disillusionment with oversimplified "How to" pieces that never really seem to work in real life, I once wrote a humorous piece titled, "Fixing a Flat in 34 Easy Steps." It was published in *Bike-Centennial.* I subsequently tried—without success—to resell the piece to other markets with the obvious biking and outdoor recreation connections. No one bit. Then, while I was working on an unrelated piece for a veteran's magazine, I learned that the magazine was sponsoring a bike tour to raise funds for a war memorial. When I mentioned my humorous how-to piece, the editor snapped it up. In checking my files, I see it was published the second time as "How to Fix a Flat in *39* Easy Steps," which suggests I either got funnier or windier in the intervening two years. This experience taught me to fish around for connections that may not be immediately obvious.

## Fillers, Factoids, and Quotes

While researching a piece about colossi as kitsch in America, I came across a price list from a company that manufactured giant fiberglass sculptures. The list included items and prices such as "Flamingo (26 ft.

high, 2,000 lbs.): $31,900"; "Cow Head, Giant (6 ft. high, 250 lbs.): $3,900"; and "Golf Bag (11½ ft. high, 600 lbs.): $9,900." I forwarded a copy of the list and a written summary of background information to an editor at *Harper's,* where it was subsequently published as a Reading. Many magazines use "fillers" and so note in their guidelines. Listings in *Writer's Market* usually indicate if a magazine is in the market for fillers. A quote or interesting fact from your article (or even one that didn't make the final cut) may be of interest to another publication.

### Jog Your Brain

Every once in a while, I pull out (or pull up, now that it's available on CD-ROM) my copy of *Writer's Market* and just read through the categories. It's a great way to trigger topical associations. Not only will you discover new markets for old material, you'll come away from these sessions filled with potential new ideas. If you share my mental retention capacity, however, make sure you make notes while doing your jogging.

### Check Your Back Files

Look through your old articles. Has anything happened since they were published that would make an update salable?

## OFFSHOOTS

Not all of the extra mileage you get from an article will spring directly from content. Instead, an assignment may set in motion a fortuitous chain of events. Way on back in 1990, I was asked to profile an up-and-coming country band for a regional magazine. While interviewing the lead singer, I learned that her husband was a world-champion lumberjack. After the band piece appeared, I sold a profile of her husband and his successful lumberjack show to the same magazine. Next, based on what I had learned from the lumberjack, I sold a piece to the *Saint Paul Pioneer-Press* on the lumberjack world championships. And then back to the band: Their drummer, a talented performer in his own right, owned a small pizza shop and a backwoods recording studio in northern

Wisconsin. Looking at the map included with writer's guidelines supplied by *Lake Superior Magazine,* I realized that the town in which his pizza parlor was located fell within the magazine's geographic target area. Based solely on the location of his pizza parlor, I pitched a profile of the drummer to the magazine, and got the assignment.

I'll stop there, but the connections continue, right down to the present. I believe that if I tracked backward from every story I write, over half would lead to the same point. Case in point: When I finished the original piece on the country band, I reslanted it and pitched it to a national magazine. The editor wrote back to say he enjoyed the piece but couldn't use it. He added, "but keep me in mind for future projects." I did, and just this year, *seven years later but still based on that initial contact,* I placed a feature with his magazine.

Let me close by saying this "fortuitous chain of events" may have had its origins in accident or chance, but it was kept alive because I had my "radar" on and acted on the leads I picked up. You'll need to do the same.

## WHAT'S THE MARKET?

The market for secondary sales is as wide as you make it. In "Seven Steps to Selling Each Article as Many Times as Possible," a piece written for the Writer's Digest publication *1,082 Tips to Write Better and Sell More!,* Dennis E. Hensley outlines how he markets his articles to publications ranging from small local newspapers to international periodicals. While payment at the local level can be as low as $5, payment at the upper end can reach four figures. What makes a $5 resale worth your time? That $5 will buy postage to submit to several of the higher-paying markets.

In some cases, the market is obvious—pitching a story about rural dating in the Midwest to a Midwestern publication with a rural readership and noncompeting geographical distribution. In other cases—recall the bike repair and bowhunting examples—the connection will not be obvious. In other cases, tangential associations are key—the colossi material that became a *Harper's* Reading, for example.

I opened this chapter by saying I don't spend enough time attending to secondary sales, and that's true. But I also have more than enough work (at the moment, tap wood), and feel my time is better spent moving on to another larger, more challenging assignment than reslanting my piece on oxygen therapy for the local weekly. If that statement sounds snobbish, forgive me. It isn't intended to. Freelancing has a way of keeping you humble. But you have to balance your desire to extract every penny from a piece with your available time and how you wish to spend it. I'd rather sacrifice a secondary sale here and there in order to develop my skills as an essayist, or take off for Central America to research a piece on displaced Confederate soldiers.

Having said that, I kept another screen active while writing this chapter; it is filled with ideas for reslanting and reselling work I've completed in the previous year. At least I know one writer who has benefited from this book!

## Know Your Rights

When a magazine buys an article, it is actually buying "rights" to that article. The nature of the rights you sell will affect your ability to resell the piece or benefit from subsequent reprintings of the piece. Before you sell a piece, inquire as to the rights you are selling, and then get the agreement to purchase those rights in writing.

Following is a listing of the rights you are likely to encounter.

**First Serial Rights.** This means the publication purchasing your article has the right to be the first periodical to publish your work. First serial rights are usually purchased for a set period of time. You retain all other rights. Once the piece appears in print and the agreed-upon time elapses, you have the right to offer the piece for sale to other publications.

**First North American Rights/First North American Serial Rights.** The same as First Serial Rights, with the exception that the rights are limited to North America.

**One-Time Rights/Simultaneous Rights.** This means the publication has purchased the nonexclusive right to publish the piece once, in its circulation area. The author is free to sell the work to other publications at the same time, usually in areas of noncompeting circulation.

**Second Serial Rights/Reprint Rights.** The publication purchasing second serial rights is purchasing the right to print work that has already appeared in another publication.

**All Rights/All World Rights.** The publication purchases exclusive and total rights to your piece. You may not resell the piece. In general, you will not benefit from subsequent reprintings or reuse of the piece, although in some cases, you may be able to get your rights reassigned. I sold all rights to a piece once: I was paid handsomely, but I also watched the piece reappear in several markets subsequent to its original publication. Would I have been financially better off had I refused the sale? Probably not, as it was the prominent placement of the piece in the first place that drew the attention it received in the second place. It's a tough call. I was hungry at the time.

**Work Made for Hire.** Watch out for this one. When you sign a work made for hire agreement, you sign away all rights, including copyright. The individual or company purchasing your work can legally publish it under the byline of anyone they wish.

**Electronic Rights.** Ever wish you were a pioneer, carving out new territory? Here's your chance. With the exponential explosion of electronic forms of media, writers run the very real risk of losing control of their work. Laws, rules, and industry standards concerning electronic rights are evolving as you read this. Terms of electronic rights have begun to spring up in my contracts, and at the moment, I can jump on the Web and track down a number of my articles. Do I receive additional compensation for these postings? Only in a very few cases. At the moment, my best advice is this: Don't sign any contract without first determining your electronic rights. Discuss them with the editor. Your power to control your electronic destiny is limited, but I've found I have some influence, and it is only through the active pursuit of these rights that we will establish acceptable standards.

This has been only a basic discussion of rights. Depending on your material, you may have to address book, movie, or TV rights. The bottom line: Be sure you understand your rights *before* you sign on the dotted line. You may also wish to study more in-depth resources. I can recommend two:

*The Basics of Selling and Protecting Your Writing.* Writer's Digest Books, 1507 Dana Avenue, Cincinnati, OH 45207.

"Showdown on the Electronic Frontier," by Howard G. Zaharoff, *Writer's Digest,* June 1996.

# CHAPTER FOURTEEN

# THE BUSINESS END

One of the things I cherish most about freelancing is my relative freedom. No set schedule, no time clock, no boss breathing down my neck, no office politics (although I have been known to engage in fairly spirited and acrimonious argument with myself, often out loud). No squinty-eyed middle manager cruising past my cubicle, no chest-thumping crew boss counting off my shovel scoops, no corporate board peering down a mile-long conference table in forceful expectation of favorable financial revelations. Nothing to do but boil some water for tea, climb the stairs to the garret, cue the CD symphony, and fill the day with soft flurries of words.

Now then. If I were a responsible author, I'd counter this wry little bundle of badinage with a stern admonition. Point out that by golly, Ms. or Mr. Would-Be Writer, you'd darn well better expect to buckle down, and if you think the freelance life is all about sipping tea and freedom and listening to Pink Floyd and Puccini at 10 A.M., well then by gosh you had better just take a ball peen hammer to those frilly little dreams of yours and get used to the fact that freelancing is a hack-eat-hack business and you are adrift in a troubled and sharky ocean aboard a leaky raft with one thin oar and you'd better just buckle down and row, row, *row* your boat!

But you see, sometimes it *is* about tea and symphony and words in the morning. And it *is* about privacy and independence. Freelancers all freelance differently. Some are superbly efficient and fastidiously organized. Others have a more haphazard approach. But in the end, you are rewarded for what you deliver. If you can deliver high quality writing in a timely manner despite a haphazard approach, you'll be rewarded just the same. Yes, there are tangible rewards to an ordered attack, and you must never forget that freelancing is a business. The same principles that make successful businesses successful will contribute to your success. But I didn't pursue life as a freelancer so that I could improve my time management skills. I pursued life as a freelancer so I could *write.* And some days, I boil water for tea, climb the stairs, and simply write.

I said in the introduction of this book that I'd be honest with you, and here's another chance to prove it. Just as I think there is a tendency in many publications to over-rhapsodize about writing, there is also a tendency to overemphasize moneymaking. We are often encouraged to listen to so-and-so because he or she earns X amount of dollars. Indeed, on one level, dollars are often a good reflection of success. I've read several books and any number of articles by freelancers anointed by virtue of their income, and there is no doubt that they know more about making money than I do. Would my financial picture be rosier if I followed all their tips? Yep. Do I consistently fail to maximize my earning potential? Without a doubt. Would it be fiscally wiser to repackage my article on skiing tips rather than spend two days revising an essay that may never sell? Certainly. But I direct your attention back one paragraph. I said I pursued *life* as a freelancer. Not a *career* as a freelancer, not a *job* as a freelancer, but *life* as a freelancer. I can't tell you what *life* is about, but you have to ask yourself that very question. Is your life more about financial security or more about writing? For most of us it's probably somewhere in between. I treat freelancing as a professional occupation when I need to—you won't survive long if you don't—but I am consumed and driven by writing. I am not consumed and driven by the number a few lines removed from the bottom of my tax return.

This isn't sniping. These comments aren't directed at the editors or authors of the pieces in question. They're directed at you. Make sure you strike your own happy medium. Be realistic, be professional, strive for financial reward, but don't wake up one morning and discover you're working for someone you don't like.

Having said these things, lets move on to our section titled "Ten Red-Hot No-Miss Tips for Streamlining Your Path to Financial Freedom!" Or at least, to discuss a few of the things you need to consider before you launch your writing raft in the sharky ocean.

## BILLING

"Writers forced to fight tooth and claw for payment": I've read the horror stories, and I know it happens, but for some reason, my experience has been fairly benign. With the exception of the commercial client referred to in Chapter Four, I can only recall being paid what I was promised.

Whenever possible, have your assignment put in writing—preferably in the form of a signed contract. Come to agreement on per diem and out-of-pocket expenses, mileage reimbursement, and kill-fee terms. Some of the editors I work with send me an agreement in the form of a purchase order.

When I submit an invoice, it's nothing fancy. I print it on my letterhead, and include:

- Date submitted.
- My social security number.
- Editor's name, name of publication, publication address. *NOTE:* Ask in advance where and to whom your bill should be sent. Several of the magazines I write for request that the invoice be sent directly to a specific individual in the accounting department. An invoice sent to the editorial department runs the risk of being lost; at the very least, payment is likely to be delayed.
- A brief description of the piece in question. Unless the piece has already hit print, I don't refer to the piece by title, as it may change. If the piece has been requisitioned through a purchase order, I include the P.O. number with the description.
- A summary of charges. Usually, my invoices consist of one line. If further breakdown is necessary, itemize and subtotal as appropriate.
- If my expenses are being reimbursed, I include photocopies of receipts or credit card billing, as well as any necessary explanation.
- Finally, a total.

Simple computerized invoicing programs are available, and may be worth the investment. In my specific experience, billing has been a very simple process, and I've never felt the need for such a program.

## WHAT IF I DON'T GET PAID?

As I mentioned in Chapter Four, I can only recall really getting burned once, and that was by a commercial client, not an editor. If you do run into collection problems with a magazine, you can follow generally the sequence outlined in Chapter Four, with a few modifications:

1. When payment is one month overdue, send a second copy of the bill, accompanied by a polite reminder. No cutesy stamps or stickers.
2. If two more weeks pass without payment, make a phone call. Speak directly to the person in charge of paying invoices (at a small magazine, it may be the editor). State your case politely and firmly. If you're told the check is in the mail or will be soon, get specifics. If the check doesn't show when it should, get back on the phone.
3. *Still* can't get paid? Chances are, you're facing the classic "blood from a turnip" scenario. If a magazine has the finances to pay you, it most likely will. Writers are mighty low in the power structure, but thriving magazines worth writing for rarely get that way by refusing to pay writers. At this point you may wish to pursue professional assistance, if financially feasible.
4. Don't forget the possibilities of a negotiated payment arrangement.

John M. Wilson suggests that if you belong to a national or sizable regional writer's organization, they may be able to bring some pressure to bear on the publication, or even provide you with limited legal support.

Wilson makes another recommendation that I can attest to. He suggests that writers who have been stiffed contact *Writer's Digest* and *Writer's Market,* as they warn writers of potentially troublesome publications. Most writing trade publications (*Freelance Success* and *ByLine,* for instance) do the same. I once avoided a potentially troublesome encounter thanks to one of these postings, and was glad someone had taken the time to spread the word. You can also spread the word rapidly through on-line writer's discussion forums and bulletin boards.

Actually, this last recommendation may be a small source of leverage if you let the editor who owes you money know of your intent. Just don't get carried away in a revenge fantasy. Don't allow vitriol to derail your professional deportment; simply state the facts, act judiciously and with good speed, and abandon revenge to the passing of time.

## TAXES

According to *Writer's Digest* contributor Peter H. Desmond, each year the IRS summons 1 percent of all the folks who declare their occupation as "writer" to see if they've earned their tax deductions. If you're one of those lucky ducks, you'll need to produce more than three limericks and a half-finished essay on dandelions to legitimize your tax status. You must be able to demonstrate that your writing activity is intended to produce a profit. If you produce a profit two out of five years, then the government presumes that the writing activity is profit motivated. The intention is the key. If someone travels all over the world, deducting all the expenses, and once or twice a year shows $100 income for an article, but in the meantime has income from another source, then the IRS is likely to disallow those deductions. This is an area of tax law filled with words like "presumption" and "intent." A gray area, to say the least. Unlike Mr. Desmond, I am not a tax expert, and this section should *not* be relied upon as sufficient in its advisory capabilities to get you out of jams with your friendly government tax collector.

At the risk of sounding glib, here's my advice on the tax front: Keep your receipts, write down your mileage, stay in your room, and hire an accountant.

Up until just a few years ago, I did my own taxes. But then a friend and I started a two-man advertising agency, and things got a bit more intricate, so we retained an accountant. As my freelance work increased, it seemed only natural to let him do my tax return, and he does to this day. He does his part, I do mine:

**Receipts.** Keep them. I have a file labeled "Receipts," and by December it bulges like a postman's bag at Christmas.

- If I mail something at the post office, I get a receipt. Before I leave the counter, I jot down what was mailed and whether I paid with cash or check.
- If I make a writing-related purchase, I keep the receipt, and jot an explanatory note on its face. If I pick up writing supplies as well as some personal items, I circle or check off deductible

items. When I'm not sure about the deductibility of an item, I make a note of it and let my accountant decide (see the "Accounting for Yourself" section).

- Keep travel-related receipts, airline ticket stubs, and so on.
- Sometimes a note supplants a receipt. For certain travel or entertainment expenses below $75, you merely need to jot down the details: when, where, why, and with whom. I still get receipts whenever possible.

**Mileage.** Put a pad of paper in your car. Every time you take a writing-related journey, note the beginning and ending mileage, the date, and why you took the trip. At tax time, you can turn those miles into money.

- Remember: if you go to the store for candy bars, cotton balls, and manuscript paper, the trip is a business trip . . . as long as the *primary* purpose was to buy manuscript paper.
- If you think of it, make a note of your mileage each New Year's Day (or so). This helps your accountant determine your total yearly mileage and establish the parameters for deduction calculations.

**Home Office Deduction.** This is the "stay in your room" bit. If your home is your principal place of business and you have a net profit (thus the reason limericks aren't enough), you can write off a certain percentage of your housing expenses as business expenses. The home office deduction game has gotten a bit more tricky in recent years, and the IRS radar has been tweaked to pick up cheaters. Basically, you will minimize your likelihood of running afoul of the law by making your work area very clearly distinct from the rest of the house. My office is in a converted bedroom. My computer, printer, scanner, supplies, desk, file cabinets, and the majority of my writing reference books are all in that room. There is little doubt that my home office claim is legitimate.

**Accountant.** I'm all for the do-it-yourself work ethic. But a good accountant is a wise investment. The investment isn't large, and you can further reduce the expense by showing up at the accountant's office in a timely manner (preferably not on April 14), with a reasonably ordered collection of simple records. I like my accountant. He's a nice guy. He fills out all those nasty forms and we talk about canoeing. A week later, he sends me a very reasonable bill, with absolutely no charge for the peace of mind. And the best part? He used to work for the IRS. He knows what goes. I send him chocolate now and then.

One last time: I am not a tax expert. Please check with a qualified accountant or the IRS itself. Some publications are available at local libraries or post offices. If you can't find what you need there, contact your regional IRS office (in the phone book's government offices listings) or call 1-800-829-1040.

## ACCOUNTING FOR YOURSELF

I have an inexpensive computer accounting program, Quicken®, that makes my life a lot simpler. Beyond tracking my savings and checking accounts, its single greatest value comes in tracking deductible expenses. The program allows me to categorize each expense as it is entered in my checking account. If I wrote a single check for a number of items, Quicken® allows me to break the amount down into as many categories as necessary. When I'm unsure of the deductibility of an expense, I simply enter it in a miscellaneous category. At the end of the year, I review this category with my accountant and he makes the necessary decisions.

Because the program memorizes transactions, the process of paying my regular bills is distilled to a session of under one hour per month. The "reconcile" function allows me to balance my checkbook in a matter of minutes. While neither of these things are directly related to writing, they provide the most precious benefit of all: more *time* for writing.

I cherish this program the most come tax time. A few clicks of the mouse, and I have a neat, meticulously ordered printout of my income and expenses for the previous year. I take the printout and a mileage report to my accountant, and he does the rest.

## YOUR WORK ENVIRONMENT

I was going to title this section "*Organizing* Your Work Environment," but I was afraid someone who knows me might come across the heading and suffer multiple rib fractures as a result of being convulsed with laughter. I am to organization what President Ford was to elegance and grace. And yet, in my own little ways, I have streamlined my attack by rendering some sort of organization to my little office.

**Desk.** I have a plain old discount chain particle board desk. It's L-shaped: my computer keyboard and screen are located on the shorter leg of the L; the longer leg has built-in shelves and serves as desk space. I like this arrangement because it allows me to spread reference materials and notes out within easy reach while typing. My printer is positioned at the angle of the L; again, within easy reach from the keyboard.

**Chair.** I bet you thought I was going to tell you to get a chair that supports your lower back, supports your arms just so, etc. No. I'm an indefensibly inveterate keyboard sloucher, and my recommendation on office chairs for the freelancer amounts to this: Get one that's comfortable. You're going to spend a lot of time in it. To all my friends in the fields of physical and occupation therapy, please spare me the letters about posture and carpal tunnel syndrome. I know, I *know.* It's just that I tried sitting up straight for awhile, but it made my neck hurt. And if my high school typing teacher could see the way I approach and attack the keyboard, she'd simply seize up and tip over.

**File Cabinets.** I have a short, two-drawer file just to the right of my computer keyboard. Because it is short and within easy reach, I place my scanner atop it. I keep my most active files in this cabinet, again because it is within easy reach. Another taller cabinet stores sample magazine copies and less active files. Because they are easily rearranged, I use hanging files. I've also learned over the years that you get what you pay for when it comes to file cabinets.

**Lighting.** In addition to the ceiling fixture, I have two gooseneck lamps attached to the desk on either side of my keyboard. Your eyes will thank you for the extra light.

**Supplies.** I keep as many supplies as possible within arm's reach—envelopes, labels, stationery, business cards, paper clips, stapler, three-hole punch, tape dispenser, stamps. It seems oversimple, but any time you don't have to get up or search for something, you'll conserve precious production time.

**Telephone.** I keep a telephone on the desk, and—you guessed it—within easy reach.

**Answering Machine/Fax.** Both answering machine and fax are integrated into my computer. Answering machines get bad-mouthed, but if you're going to freelance, you'll need one. I'm on the road a lot; the odds of an editor catching me in vary depending on the type of project I'm working on. I have a reputation for scrupulously returning my calls, and I've never had an editor complain about "getting a machine." Make sure you can access your messages from the road. I still have my old cassette answering machine, by the way. I keep it in a drawer for those times when my computer quits, or when I have to record a phone interview.

**Decor.** How you decorate your work area is up to you. I've opted for the prodigious accumulation of personally relevant kitsch. The walls are covered with bits of flotsam and jetsam that remind me of where I've been and why I write. From laminated press passes to Neil Diamond tickets, if I can stick it to the wall, I do. I do *not* paper the walls with rejection slips, although I have posted a handful of particularly memorable turn-downs, including one in which a publisher indicates her firm will not be interested in my material "unless your reputation as an entertainer reaches the level of Garrison Keillor. . . ." She'll be the first person I call.

## IS IT REALLY A JOB?

"It must be great, being your own boss." Yes, but you oughta try getting any work out of the wastrel who works for me. "Oh, it must be great to set your own hours, take off whenever you want to!" Yes, and come back to find that absolutely nothing has been accomplished in my absence. "You get to do such interesting things!" Yes, like buy my own health insurance.

I once heard a radio interview in which a self-employed person was asked for the secret to successful self-employment. His reply? "Wake up scared every morning."

No doubt about it, freelancing is a job, with little or no long-term security.

But whenever I get even the slightest twinge of martyrization, I grab myself by the scruff of my neck and make myself look around and back. I've picked rock in the rain. I've worked as a nurse. I've punched a clock. Freelancing may be a job, but it's a privileged existence. Writing is a craft, and in some cases a calling. But it shouldn't be confused with a *higher* calling. Whenever I begin to take on highfalutin writing airs, I think about my colleagues in nursing, still showing up, shift after shift, to care for grandmothers with strokes, fathers with spinal cord trauma, young children with head injuries. I think of all the people doing the real work, doing the tangible things that support us all, and I am rightfully humbled.

So, yes. Freelancing is a "job." If you pursue the vocation, it isn't likely you'll spend much time lost in the rapture of creation, sipping tea and flinging flurries of words to the ages. It is likely you will work harder, longer hours than anyone might suspect.

But you will have nothing to complain about.

# CHAPTER FIFTEEN

# A MELANGE OF TIPS

I've always wanted to use the word *melange,* and I believe this is my chance. This chapter, my friends, is a melange. A melange of insights, tips, tidbits, hints, unrelated miscellany, incidentals, and hard-won wisdom. A personal collectanea.

Browse at will, whilst I pour cool water over my thesaurus.

## CALCULATED CHUTZPAH

Allow me to set the scene: I had been freelancing for all of nine months. Several months previous, a well-respected and neatly executed regional magazine had published my first article. Shortly afterward, the magazine changed hands. Under new management, the magazine continued to accept my manuscripts on a regular basis. This was pleasing. However, I soon noticed that the change in ownership was followed by a deterioration in editorial quality. Typos abounded. Many of the articles were disjointed or poorly written. While I was pleased to have a paying outlet for my work, I was concerned about the image of the magazine. More to the point, I was concerned that if the quality remained poor, subscriptions and ad sales would take a hit and this precious little market for my writing would disappear. Furthermore, I saw an opportunity to pick up some additional freelance income. When an issue arrived in the mail riddled with over fifty typographical errors, chutzpah struck. I composed and mailed the following letter (names and identifying details have been changed):

Fred Smith
Publisher
*Regional Magazine*

Mr. Smith:

My grandfather was a very successful businessman. In the years since his retirement, he has become more of a friend than a grandfather to me. One of the philosophies he has passed on to me is this: "Don't approach me with a problem. Approach me with a solution."

It is from this frame of reference that I approach you today. The most recent issue of *Regional Magazine* sports a new look, which I find attractive. Unfortunately, it also sports an abundance of typographical errors.

I do not submit this observation in the form of criticism, but rather in a spirit of concern. You see, I have a vested interest in your success. I have been published several times by *Regional Magazine,* and I am grateful for these opportunities. Naturally, I want them to continue. However, I fear the results of delivering a product to the public that contains as many "clinkers" as this one, especially since the magazine is in the process of trying to court advertisers and subscribers.

"So then," you say, "what about this grandfather-induced philosophy of yours? Do you have a solution?" Well, I just may.

*(Continued)*

As you know, Mr. Smith, I work at Federal Seminar Services, Inc. The majority of my responsibilities at FSS center around proofreading. I proof hundreds of items monthly, from brochures to news releases to ad copy. I think that putting my skills to work for your magazine on a very part-time basis would result in a full-time improvement.

I would greatly appreciate the opportunity to discuss this idea with you. I will also gladly obtain references from my superiors if you wish. Please feel free to call me at the number below.

Sincerely,
Michael Perry

How was that again? "putting my skills to work for your magazine on a very part-time basis would result in a full-time improvement"!? Good grief.

The upshot of the deal was, I got the job. Next issue, I was listed in the masthead as providing "editorial services"; essentially, I was a glorified proofreader. As well as proofing copy, I assisted with rewrites in consultation with the standing editor. The experience was invaluable. Not only was I supplementing my writing income, I was learning valuable lessons on the job. The process of copyediting other writers taught me volumes about my own writing. Through my work with the editors (one new editor per issue, for a while), I gained an appreciation for their experience—an appreciation that has served me well in my dealings with editors to this day.

## CHUTZPAH, PART II

A short time after I was retained as a copyeditor at *Regional Magazine,* I happened upon a copy of a local business journal. Aha! Typos! Out came the *Regional Magazine* letter. Zip, zap, change of address, salutation, and a few other details, and in the mail it went. Sure enough, a few days later, the phone rang: It was the editor of the business journal. He made brief reference to the typos, something along the lines of "thanks for pointing that out," then said he'd take care of the problem in-house, thanks. But next, rather than tell me to get a hobby and quit firing off smart-alecky letters at the drop of a consonant, he offered me a chance to write weekly features for the journal.

I accepted, and never mentioned typos again.

Not every editor is going to sit still and be subjected to this method of job hunting. Obviously, I got lucky. I also knew the limit of my abilities. I wasn't firing these letters off to *The New Yorker.* But with a little luck, a sharp eye, and a measure of tact (I would suggest a greater measure than I employed), you might be able to supplement your freelance writing income by copyediting. Perhaps the larger lesson is this: Take a chance now and then. Invest a stamp. (It's much easier to sustain audacity in writing than over the phone, or—heaven forbid—in person. If I tried to pull this stunt off in person, I'd lock right up!)

## NO THANKS, I'LL CALL BACK

Perky receptionists or snazzy voice mail systems notwithstanding, whether you're calling to speak with an editor or to arrange an interview with a story source, do what you can to avoid leaving a message. The ratio of I'll-have-him-call-you-backs to actual returned calls is abominably low. Leave a message if you must, but don't leave it at that. Polite, persistent call-backs are your best bet.

## AT THE TONE . . .

Personally, I think people who use an answering machine to screen calls are rude. I think writers who turn their ringer off and answering machine on in order to get some uninterrupted writing done are wise. Your being unavailable because you're completing an important project under deadline is no different than a corporate executive being unavailable because she is in an important meeting. I don't recommend you make a practice of it (why frustrate an editor unnecessarily?), but using your answering machine to "hold all my calls," is a wise move if you require an uninterrupted block of time.

On a technological note, this technique hasn't worked for me ever since I got my new computer system. My telephone and answering machine are integrated with the computer, and when the phone rings—even if the ringer is turned off and the computer sound system is shut down—a little operator icon pops up on screen. Since I'm one of those people who can't let a message remain unread, or my mail go a day without pickup, when that icon pops up, I invariably answer the phone.

## LET YOUR COMPUTER WORK FOR YOU

Take advantage of time-saving computer functions. For instance, I have a "template" file set up to fit my letterhead. Margins, centering, spacing, font—they're all set. I just open the file, save it under a new name, and start typing.

I also use "macros" whenever I can. A macro is defined by my word processor's "Help" glossary as "a file containing a series of commands that help automate a task." For example, one of my biggest time-savers is an envelope macro. Activated with a click of the mouse, the envelope macro does all the setup for printing envelopes, including printer formatting and return address information. I simply paste an address in place, select "print," and move on.

Rather than painstakingly hand print addresses on large manila envelopes that won't feed through your printer, set up and save a word-processing template file formatted for mailing labels. As you finish your cover or query letter, paste the address to the label file. If you're sending out a number of envelopes, you'll save even more time by printing all the addresses at once. Then simply peel them off and stick them on. The U.S. Postal Service, by the way, prefers mail addressed in all-capital, simple block letters—they are more easily read by automated equipment.

Rather than feed envelopes through the printer one at a time, I preprint sheets of adhesive labels with my return address. Whenever I need a SASE, I simply reach for an envelope, slap a sticker and stamp in place, and away it goes.

# BACK IT UP

If you use a computer, for gosh sakes, perform regular backup procedures. I recently experienced my first "crash," and I am here to tell you that the feeling I had when the screen went blank was similar to the one I get when I realize I was supposed to pay my taxes yesterday. I had been performing intermittent backups, but I got lazy. And so, I gently detached the CPU from the monitor, tucked it in the front seat of my car (seat belt and all), and bundled it off to the computer hospital. Over the next few days (I was in the middle of an article due on deadline), I plinked away on an old laptop, and made frightened little phone calls to the computer hospital to see how surgery was going. There was much slinging of lingo. I understood none of it, save the fact that everything I had written for the past seven years was in limbo.

In the end, the spirit in the machine turned benevolent. A lingo-slinger called, and amidst all the acronyms and apparent references to numerology, I gathered that—Glory Be!—my work had been preserved. The scene in the computer store lobby was reminiscent of the sort of thing you see when a child who has been wandering around a grizzly bear preserve for three days and nights is returned alive to his parents. I was urged by those in attendance not to shed tears of joy on the disk drive.

Immediately thereafter, I proceeded to a computer super store with my cousin, an official computer magus, and picked out a backup system. Now I perform a backup (nearly) every day. I sleep well.

A few things to keep in mind:

- If you are using a word processing program, set the automatic timed backup so that your work is saved a minimum of every five minutes.
- Get in the habit of backing up your timed backup. Every time I stop typing, every time I switch screens or utilities, I try to remember to save my work in progress.
- When I'm working on a large project (this book, for instance), I save a copy of the text on a floppy disk. If my hard drive crashes, I have not only saved the work, I'm able to continue work on another computer while mine is being repaired.

- Keep two sets of backup disks. It's not unusual for a floppy disk to get temperamental. Imagine your despair should your one and only precious backup present you with a phrase along the lines of, "unable to read. . . ."
- Get paranoid. I have *three* sets of backup disks: one stored at my desk, one stored in a fire safe in my basement (not all fire safes are rated to protect computer disks, by the way), and one stored at another office forty miles from here. Obviously, I don't drive eighty miles a day to switch backup disks, but when business takes me to the other office, I take a current backup along and make the switch then. You don't have to drive forty miles, but it is a good idea to put some geographic separation between sets of backup materials to protect against catastrophes the likes of fire, flooding, tornado, hurricane, or plagues of digital locusts. (*Writer's Digest* columnist David Fryxell refers to the performance of duplicative backups as "justifiably paranoid.")

One additional note. The backup system I secured after my crash works through an add-on device called a Zip® drive. Compared to the standard 1.44 MB diskettes I had been using for backup, Zip® drive disks contain 100 MB of memory. This means I can back up my entire system (word processing, accounting, message storage, phone system address files, etc.) on one disk. Backup on the 100 MB Zip® disk takes roughly four minutes; I put a disk in, click an icon, go brush my teeth, and when I return the backup is complete. I'm here to tell you that I am now a paragon of backup virtue simply because the process is so quick and simple. I recommend you explore similar options.

## STUCK?

Sometimes the best thing you can do for your writing is to remove yourself from your writing environment. For instance, I have developed many an article lead while out on my bike or on a long run. Once I settle into the rhythm of a solid pace, I work the angles over and over in my head. Increased blood flow seems to engender increased idea flow. It's also good mental exercise: Because I can't type or jot down everything that springs to mind, I'm forced to memorize it. The process of memorization often serves a purpose similar to that of rewriting.

You don't have to exert yourself for a change of scene. I occasionally travel to a certain coffee shop to prewrite and rewrite. In the case of rewriting, I find it useful to read my work in a different setting. I seem to notice things I've missed in the office. In the case of prewriting, well, it's just plain pleasant to sift through sheafs of interview transcripts and research while sitting in a 1960s-vintage armchair with a double Americano at hand.

I do not, by the way, do much actual *writing* outside my office. I will write in public when I need to (in a journal on a train, or while covering an event, for instance), but it is my closely held belief that writers in coffee houses and other public places churn out far more pose than prose.

## WRITER'S CONFERENCES

I have been to exactly one writer's conference. Centered around the topic of creative nonfiction, it was immensely helpful, quietly invigorating, and ultimately profitable. And yet, I remain leery of the concept of writer's conferences in general. I only attended the nonfiction conference after carefully comparing it to other offerings.

Before you sign up for a conference, examine your reasons for attending. Are you interested in bolstering your writing skills, or are you interested in socializing with people of like interests? Is the content relevant? Who are the faculty? What is their level of involvement? (Beware the marquee name used to lure you across the country for a twenty-minute reading.) How is the conference structured? Will there be workshops? Critique sessions? Lectures? Readings? Is this the first time the conference has been held?

Once you decide to go, prepare. Review any materials sent in advance. Think again about your reasons for attending. Keep the time completely clear; don't plan on using your evenings and break times to work on projects that should have been left at home. Do take a journal—in addition to the obvious lecture notes, you will find that all that writing talk will fuel your creative fires.

Finally—and I think this is the most important thing to keep in mind about attending a writing conference—don't simply settle for temporary invigoration. Act, act, act. Conferences and seminars are famous for "reenergizing" the people in attendance. During breaks, everyone chatters excitedly about new insights and validations. But conferences are almost as well known for the letdown attendees experience upon their return home. You must maintain your momentum, follow through on contacts made, put new insights into practice.

I am normally quite poorly organized, but I outdid myself at my one conference. Each evening, I made a list of new contacts and markets that had come to my attention during the day. I also listed essay and article ideas that came to mind as a result of discussions and lectures. When I returned home, I forced myself to follow up on every one of the contacts and markets within two weeks. As a result, I cracked several new markets.

I also set about developing my idea list. Two of the items turned into published works. Note that these were both benefits above and beyond the bevy of functional and inspirational information I received regarding the craft of creative nonfiction.

So . . . choose your conferences carefully. Enjoy the little emotional bump you'll receive by associating with fellow travelers. But most of all, keep the conference in session long after you return home.

## GRANDMA'S GOT A RED PEN

Writers have a terrible time writing letters. Rather than dash off a note to a friend, a writer writes and rewrites, scribing away under the weight of knowing that whatever is mailed must live up to the recipient's idea of the sort of thing a *writer* would produce. Heck, my own grandma once pointed out an "i before e" type misspelling on the back of a postcard I sent her. I bet she wouldn't do the same thing to my brother the tractor mechanic. Perhaps she feared such loose behavior would result in professional censure and revocation of my license. I am further intimidated when I read the collected correspondence of celebrated giants of literature . . . didn't these people *ever* generate a mundane line? Comment on the commonplace . . . post a platitude . . . wish for better weather?

This sense of intimidation carries over to journal writing. When I have a fresh idea, observation, or insight, I often scribble it on the nearest piece of paper; if I'm at the computer, I peck it out on the fly. The resulting notes are frequently simplistic, cast in a literary form I refer to as "yearbook prosaic." When I go back through these notes, I often wince. What if someone ever unearthed this stuff? And yet, when it comes time to mine these notes, the substance of the original thought is always there, simplistic and wide-eyed though it may be.

The moral of the story? 'Tis better to get it down dumb than never get it down at all. Have an idea? Scribble it. Suffer an epiphany? Note so in simple nouns and verbs. If you develop the concept further, you can return to render it ornate at a later date. Otherwise, leave the post-mortal tidying up to your biographers and grandmother; write freely.

## CARRY A PENCIL

> "A man would do well to carry a pencil in his pocket and write down the thoughts of the moment. Those that come unsought for are commonly the most valuable, and should be secured, because they seldom return."
>
> —*Roger Bacon*

Roger Bacon probably never came home at the end of the day and pulled a wad of crumpled Post-It® notes out of his vestments, but he apparently performed the historically equivalent exercise. Many writers travel with a pen and pad as constant companion. I'm rarely that organized. But I do have a rather extensive collection of the aforementioned Post-It® notes (furred with lint from my jeans pockets, as I stopped wearing vestments years ago), triangular corners torn from magazines, notated receipt backs, and the odd candy bar wrapper, all with my scribbles on them. Writers are constantly scrounging for ideas, story seeds, apt phrases, pithy quotes, anything that can be dragooned into service and sold. My best ideas rarely arrive while I'm seated at the keyboard. Wherever I am, I'm ready (if not prepared) to commit notes to paper (since memory consistently fails me) and pocket them. Writerly histrionics are unnecessary, by the way. If you insist on reeling back, smacking yourself across the forehead, and uttering stunned "Eurekas" every five minutes or so, you'll find it difficult to sustain friendships, keep work, or shoot a decent game of pool. A discreet jot will do.

## THE POWER OF BOREDOM

America has a phobia for boredom. The frenetic pursuit of its alleviation leads to all manner of cultural phenomena: Wave after wave of video games, legions of cable channels, Internet chat[ter] rooms, line dancing, the revivification of the 1970s . . . all in the interest of artificially stimulating our synapses so there will be no room for the pariah boredom.

If you wish to be a writer, I suggest you accord boredom a little more respect.

There is something about boredom that stimulates creativity. And a new variation on the Boot-Scoot doesn't have to be the result. Earlier, I mentioned my collection of Post-It® notes. I scribbled and pocketed most of them while trolling for dropped semicolons in a never-ending raft of probate attorney bios. I got more inspiration to write from sitting through interminable, dehydrated university lectures than I ever have on those occasions when I sit down with a blank page and plenty of time to write. I suspect that part of the reason we so desperately wish we were back at home with our word processor at times like these is precisely because we can't be. We always want what we can't have, right?

We are most ambitious and creative when we are dissatisfied. Boredom is a form of dissatisfaction. When the clock seems to have stripped its gears, our mind fidgets like a child, churning out wishful alternatives to the situation at hand—a way out of boredom. It is a perverse characteristic of human nature that when a block of free time presents itself, your mind is likely to lapse into a low torporific hum. So welcome boredom. Trust it to lead you to fertile ground. And be prepared to take notes.

## THINK IN PROSE

This is a tough concept for me to articulate. It's also tough to describe without coming off as overly consumed or dramatic. But I'll give it a shot. When I'm out and about, I try to describe the things I sense. Sounds, sights, shapes, whatever springs to mind. I imagine that I will need to describe this scene to someone later, and that my description will need to be evocative; that it must leave the listener with a distinct picture of what I saw.

An example: The first time I heard Dwight Yoakam sing "Long White Cadillac," I was struck by a vocal stunt he pulled in the opening line. He broke a note with a yodel, but it was more than that. More violent. A swift fracture of sound. And yet, committing vocal whiplash, he reversed direction, landing right back in tune. And so I worried the words around in my head, trying to find a way to describe the sound to someone who had never heard it. Finally I settled on describing his voice as snapping through the yodel the way a silken ribbon snaps in the wind. I wasn't writing about Dwight Yoakam, and until now the phrase has never seen print, but I enjoyed the mental tussle. I view this exercise as a sort of mental calisthenics, a way to sharpen your skills on the move.

Try not to perform this calisthenics out loud on the bus.

## POETRY AS PROSE

I am not a poet. I love to write poetry, and I approach it with a great deal of determination and attention, but I know poets, and I am not a poet. My poetry is better described as short lines in a stack. Why do I persist? First, because it is an abiding visceral pleasure. Second, because the writing of poetry can pay great dividends toward the crafting of prose.

The poet and nonfiction writer Diane Ackerman has described her experience of having nonfiction pieces arise from her poetry. She refers to the resulting essays as "unrequited poems." I can't say that I've turned an "unrequited poem" into a complete essay, but I can go back through any number of pieces and point out phrases that originated as lines of poetry.

I recently attended a semester-long poetry workshop at a local university, and I was pleasantly surprised at how easily the lessons I learned there transferred to my prose writing. There is something about writing in the mode of poet that encourages us to make connections we might never make as a prose writer. With a poetic mindset we seem more willing to experiment with unusual arrangements and combinations of words. Therefore, I encourage all writers to spend time writing "short lines in a stack."

## SIGNS YOU MAY BE PROCRASTINATING

"Without pressure, the work sometimes doesn't get done at all."
—*William Saran, quoted in* Writer's Yearbook 1962

We live in a procrastinator's world. Fax machines, cellular phones, overnight delivery services, e-mail; if we speak in the jargon of therapy, we would classify these things "enablers." The last minute has finally become just that.

How do you overcome procrastination? By dawdling around over articles on how to overcome procrastination, the cynic in me wants to say. The practical guy in me says, by enforcing as much order on your approach to writing as possible, and I have offered some tips to that effect in this book. But the honest, straightforward guy in me says, I'm not sure you ever do. It's a pathetic, regrettable habit that ages you prematurely and puts your reputation at risk. But it also seems to fuel some writers' strongest writing. There is something about pressure that enables us to train our energies on the task at hand with complete, sustained focus.

Procrastination is every writer's devil. Based on my experience, here are some signs that you may be engaged in procrastination.

- Not only is the house spotless, you've vacuumed the curtains.
- You're reworking the third draft of a letter to an aunt you haven't seen or felt the need to correspond with since 1987.
- You've ironed all the Kleenex.
- You're crushing aluminum cans . . . at 3 A.M.
- It's off to the coffee shop for half a pound of Tanzanian Teaberry; suddenly the Taster's Choice instant decaf simply won't do.
- Hooray! Finally got those K-Tel albums alphabetized!

## CRITICISM

"I would rather be attacked than unnoticed. For the worst thing you can do to an author is to be silent as to his works. An assault upon a town is a bad thing; but starving it is still worse."
—*Samuel Johnson*

I like criticism. If someone takes the time to criticize your writing, they have (usually) taken time to *read* your writing. Viewed in that light, criticism—positive or negative—is a thing to be sought after. As a freelancer, you'll get criticism from readers, editors, fellow writers, and—if you're making the right kind of waves—*critics.*

Criticism is valuable in that it forces us to step outside our own frame of reference and regard our writing from the point of view of the reader, often in the comparative context of other writing. Just as we may fail to notice a quirky personal habit until someone draws our attention to it, we often fail—from our perspective *within* the writing—to see the weaknesses, the cliched moves, the unconscious patterns we tend to fall into time and time again as writers.

Of course, the motivations of the critic deserve some examination. As important as it is for you to turn criticism to your advantage, you must also have enough strength of vision to know when to disregard it. The easiest criticism to respond to is criticism of your mechanics; basically, you're either doing it right, or you're doing it wrong. Criticism of your style is a different circumstance entirely. Will you change your approach just because it doesn't suit someone's fancy? As important as it is to listen to criticism with an open mind, it is equally important for you to possess a vision of where you are and where you wish to be as a writer. Let's get grand:

> "The author himself is the best judge of his own performance; none has so deeply meditated on the subject; none is so sincerely interested in the event."
>
> —*Edward Gibbon*

The more you learn about your own writing, the more willing you are to hold it up to brutal scrutiny, the more likely it will begin to take on that character that will render it not just readable, but distinctive.

# CHAPTER SIXTEEN

# RESOURCES

Resources for the writer are abundant. Their practical utility varies. You must glean what you can wherever you can. The more resources you read, the longer you're in the business, the less likely you are to discover new information, but I still scan new material. The process is like panning for gold—you have to move a lot of gravel for a fleck of the good stuff, but it's worth looking for.

The resource list that follows is eclectic, and based on my experience. It is by no means comprehensive; nor is it intended to be.

## BOOKS FOR FREELANCE WRITERS

***Writer's Market*** (F&W Publications, 1507 Dana Avenue, Cincinnati, OH 45207). An annual compilation of magazine and publisher listings. I have made a number of sales as a result of leads uncovered within its pages; since 1990 it has been an annual investment that has more than paid for itself.

Annually updated editor and writer interviews, and straightforward, hype-free sections including "Getting Published," and "The Business of Writing," provide mini-courses in how to go about the business of freelancing. The breakdown of consumer and trade magazines by subject is most helpful when targeting queries.

As extensive as *Writer's Market* listings are, they are not comprehensive. Don't neglect other market sources, including the *Literary Market Place, National Directory of Magazines,* and market listings in writing newsletters and trade magazines. Also keep in mind that by the time you read the information in *Writer's Market,* it is necessarily dated.

A quick phone call to verify editor names, mailing addresses, etc., is a good idea.

As of 1997, *Writer's Market* is available on CD-ROM.

**John M. Wilson, *The Complete Guide to Magazine Article Writing*** (Writer's Digest Books, an imprint of F&W Publications, 1507 Dana Avenue, Cincinnati, OH 45207). "Complete" is right. This is an excellent book. You'll need more information about freelancing in general if you expect to survive, but when it comes to writing for magazines, Wilson has written an interesting, comprehensive, and eminently practical guide.

**Bob Bly, *Secrets of a Freelance Writer: How to Make $85,000 a Year*** (Bob Bly, 22 E. Quackenbush Avenue, Dumont, NJ 07628). On my copy of this book, I circled the subtitle and wrote, "Go to medical school!" However, when it comes to sharing information that will help you survive as a freelancer until the time when you are retained exclusively by *Harper's* and *The New Yorker* to write contemplative essays, Bly's book is packed with usable goods. Especially useful in the development of commercial writing business. One of my early staples.

***1,082 Tips to Write Better and Sell More!*** (F&W Publications, 1507 Dana Avenue, Cincinnati, OH 45207). A special one-off magazine published by the folks at *Writer's Digest.* This collection of how-to advice is a nice distillation of lessons that will save you a lot of time and heartache. Despite the punctuation of the title and the use of subtitles the likes of "How to Provide Articles That Editors Can't Refuse," the hyperbole meter reads fairly low throughout. Worth tracking down.

**Lisa Collier Cook, *How to Write Irresistible Query Letters*** (Writer's Digest Books, an imprint of F&W Publications, 1507 Dana Avenue, Cincinnati, OH 45207). A generous selection of examples and advice to help you develop the esoteric art of the successful query.

**Don McKinney, *Magazine Writing That Sells*** (Writer's Digest Books, an imprint of F&W Publications, 1507 Dana Avenue, Cincinnati, OH 45207). A fine complement to Wilson's *Complete Guide.*

**Robert W. Bly, *Careers for Writers & Others Who Have a Way with Words*** (VGM Career Horizons, 4255 West Touhy Avenue, Lincolnwood, IL 60646-1975). A useful overview that will help you expand your writing vision beyond magazines.

**Arthur Plotnik, *Honk If You're a Writer*** (Fireside). I came across *Honk If You're a Writer* about one week before I finished the text of the book you're reading. I wish I'd found it years ago. I cherish Plotnik's irreverent take, his willingness to prick the balloons of pretension and disclose the convoluted truth about writing. Read it, and I expect you'll laugh and learn.

## MAGAZINES AND NEWSLETTERS

***Freelance Success*** (Judith Broadhurst, 270 Brown Gables Road, Ben Lomond, CA 95005; e-mail: 74774.1740@compuserve.com). Pithy, frank, and refreshingly free of cheerleading. Editor Broadhurst calls'em as she sees'em. Excellent market information. Available via snail mail or e-mail. Well worth the subscription.

***Writer's Digest*** (F&W Publications, 1507 Dana Avenue, Cincinnati, OH 45207). If you can get past an editorial tone that tends toward overoptimistic hyperbole, you will find much of use in this old standard (born in 1920 as *Successful Writing*). I've landed an assignment or two from the monthly market section, and when publishers, editors, or agents are being more naughty than nice, you're likely to hear about it in "The Markets." My bottom-line recommendation? Every year I say I won't renew; every year I do.

December issue, ***Writer's Digest.*** Each December issue of *Writer's Digest* includes an annual subject index, grouping all the articles of the previous year by topic.

***Harper's, The Atlantic, DoubleTake,*** etc. A resource doesn't necessarily have to be didactic. I read these publications because they educate me. They raise the bar. I leave their pages knowing there is work to be done . . . I have miles to go.

***Editor & Writer*** (Blue Dolphin Press, 83 Boston Post Road, Sudbury, MA 01776). Just debuted, incorporating *Writing for Money* and *Assignments*. So far, this has been a useful source.

## ONLINE RESOURCES

While I use the Internet and Web fairly actively, I haven't availed myself of many of the numerous writing resources to be found there. I have made a quick visit to *Editor & Publisher* magazine's Website at http://www.mediainfo.com:80/edpub/ep/classi.htm, and I've also swung by The Monster Board at http://199.94.216.71:80/home.html. I was directed to both of these sites by "Working the Web," an article by Skip Press in the August, 1996 issue of *Writer's Digest.*

From the theoretical to the functional, resources on writing abound. Subscribe to the right magazine and soon you'll be on a mailing list that will have entire catalogs on books devoted to writing stacking up in your mailbox. Swing by your local library, look in the catalog under writing, and you'll find a raft of titles. Run an Internet search and you'll uncover another dimension of writing resources.

And remember: By definition, a resource is something that can be used for support or help. Use what you can,but don't force yourself into a mold of someone else's design.

## CONCLUSION

Well, that's one way to do it.

No matter how many how-to articles declare otherwise, no one can write a universal ten-step guide to freelance success. It's a nuanced, wonderfully tricky business, with few constants. Talent takes you dancing, but perseverance buys your shoes. Luck and chance play their part. You are the greatest intangible in the equation, the most critical variable.

If, at times in the chapters past, I have seemed brusque or flip, I hope you have seen beyond the informality of my voice to the depth at which I love this business of writing. It is immensely rewarding, ultimately satisfying, and never old. With each step down the path I see more clearly just how far I have to go.

It's been a fine journey. May it be the same for you.

MIAMI-DADE COMMUNITY COLLEGE
MIAMI, FLA.
DEMCO